You Are Creative!

You Are Creative!

TURN YOUR IDEAS INTO REALITY IN 15 MINUTES A DAY

Ghylenn Descamps

Get Creative 6

"CREATIVITY IS OXYGEN
FOR OUR SOULS."

—Julia Cameron, author of
The Artist's Way

Introduction

Do you wish you could let that little creative spark inside of you flourish into something wonderful? Or do you want to get more creative, but can't figure out how to make that happen? Maybe you already started out on something creative, but right now it is a half-finished project that's gotten buried in a bottom drawer. Or you don't know quite where to begin. Do you even think of yourself as creative? Maybe you don't believe you're up to it, or you don't have enough time, or you feel it would not really be your thing. But do you look at creative people and wish that was you? Do you want to put creativity right at the heart of your life? Or learn more about the process, bringing something practical and creative into your life? Perhaps you have already made a start, but want to grow your creativity into a richer and more fruitful experience.

WHEREVER YOU ARE ON YOUR OWN CREATIVE JOURNEY, THIS BOOK HAS BEEN WRITTEN FOR YOU!!

I BELIEVE

I BELIEVE THAT EACH AND EVERY ONE OF US IS UNIQUELY CREATIVE.

Perhaps your creativity is buried deep within you, so you're simply unaware of it. But it remains in there, within reach, ready to be awoken. Whatever your past history, there was a time in your life when you were a creative little kid. If you give a three-year-old some crayons, they'll start creating something, no questions asked. So of course you too were creative in your childhood: ready to play with whatever came your way: a leaf, a feather, a lump of sugar, even maybe a snail. But you probably don't remember any of this.

I BELIEVE THAT THANKS TO YOUR CREATIVITY, YOU HAVE A UNIQUE STORY TO TELL.

Who says creativity is something only artists can enjoy? You have creative talents that can flourish in every aspect of your life. And you have an incredible potential to be creative that exists right through to your core. Your creativity is unique to you, so you have a creativity that nobody else can possess. Across all of humanity, our creativity is distinct and individual to each one of us, in part fashioned by our personality, background, tastes, and emotions, making it truly unique to ourselves.

I BELIEVE THAT WE CAN ALL FIND OUR OWN SOURCE OF INSPIRATION.

Creativity has a place for everyone: a place where we can all shine in our own distinct way. Being creative meets a deeply felt need in all of us to express something about who we are.

I BELIEVE THAT IF YOU DON'T CREATE, YOU'RE DENYING THE WORLD A CHANCE TO SEE THE BEAUTY THAT IS IN YOU.

If you don't share your inner creativity, there can be a sense that something has closed down, as if you're waiting for something, somewhere, to get started. But by managing, somehow, to express your creativity, you're reconnecting with your inner self, bringing your own colors and textures out and into the world. You allow yourself to be seen and allow others to experience you, to get to know you, and be inspired by you. The world *needs* your creativity.

When I stop and think just how much my own creativity makes me happy, feeds my soul, brings me out of myself, teaches me to know myself, accept myself, and show myself to others, then it makes me want more than anything to invite you on this journey: to share what I have experienced and show how you can be creative too.

CREATIVITY IS LIKE A GOLDEN THREAD THAT WILL LEAD YOU TO YOUR INNER SELF. FOR ME, IT MAKES ME FEEL WHOLE AND ENRICHES EVERY DAY OF MY LIFE. WHICH IS WHY I WANT TO SHARE THIS WITH YOU.

This book is based on a simple principle: give your creativity a workout, one day at a time, and it will start to blossom. This is why I have organized the book over 365 individual days: enough time to embark on a gentle and steady journey toward your inner self. Immersing yourself in creativity, day by day, will allow you to develop new ways of thinking. Ultimately, this will leave you feeling happier and more enthusiastic, with a sense of "letting go" of what was holding you back. You will start to find a place for your creativity, so it can take a role in changing your life for the better, as you sow the seeds of new ideas and feel the creative energy flowing. You may find yourself discovering completely new things, or revisiting old projects that you cast aside, seeing them in a new way. This is a journey of discovery of your own self, and a means of drawing on some of your finest—and perhaps deeply hidden—qualities.

My aim for the book is to accompany you, day by day, on this creative journey, giving you a series of themes to think about to allow you to discover what really resonates with your own experiences. All along the way you can make your own choices, dropping anything you feel is not speaking directly to you and moving on to the themes that do. The idea is to let your natural creativity emerge, raw, unfiltered, and beautiful—for your own well-being and for the happiness of those in your life.

Of course, this is a book that will take you a whole year to read, and will require a certain investment of time on your part: around 15 minutes each day on average. With a life full to the brim with family, work, and everything else, this may already seem like a big ask. But just take a moment to think about what you might gain as a result. By making this special time for you to connect with your own creativity, you're doing yourself—and also your family and your friends—a huge favor: by becoming more yourself, more centered, and happy. And by showing them that creativity is helping you, by nourishing a vital part of your being and making you feel more complete, you will inspire those around you to do the same.

HOW TO GET THE MOST OUT OF THIS BOOK

First, be yourself and have fun! Think of your passion and enthusiasm as if they were muscles, and you're going to tone them up at the creativity gym by getting into stuff that you love and that is going to light up your life.

Second, try to keep to one exercise each day. All the exercises are designed to take around 15 minutes of your time. If you give yourself this amount of time over a whole year, imagine the progress you'll make! If you miss a day, don't worry, but try as much as you can to keep up the daily routine. Some exercises take more time than others, and you can always switch them around if that helps. After all, this is your program, and you're in charge.

Third, don't put yourself under any pressure. The whole point of this is to find your inner source of creativity and release it into your life. It's not a competition. Be mindful of your own well-being, and aim to be nonjudgmental, patient, and kind to yourself all the way through.

Finally, you now need to start thinking of yourself as the coauthor of this book. Without your participation, the book is not complete, so now it's over to you: it's your book, for you to write, so make it come alive!

FINALLY, I'D LIKE YOU TO PLACE CREATIVITY AT THE HEART OF YOUR LIFE. AS JULIA CAMERON PUTS IT:

CREATIVITY IS OXYGEN
FOR OUR SOULS.

I'd like you to choose a kind of creativity that will make you happy. A positive kind of creativity that becomes addictive to your well-being, and that will allow you to see life in a new way, bringing you joy, poetry, and enthusiasm. I'd like you to experience magical, inspirational moments where everything seems possible, as if your hands know exactly what there is to do and where your mind is little more than an interested spectator. I'd like you to feel like you're riding a wave in the present moment, basking in pleasure where time is absent and your heart sings! I'd love for you to be able to experience these moments, which are the apex of the creative life.

 I want you to take back your creative power and decide to make it part of your life. From here on in, it's up to you!

WEEK 1

Getting started

· HELLO ·

READY FOR A
CREATIVE
ADVENTURE ?

· HELLO ·

DAY 1

Let's go!

Today marks the beginning of a new life with creativity at its heart. It's a big day, and a big moment. You're setting out on a journey to find your own unique brand of creativity, which will involve making discoveries about yourself. It's a huge deal!

It's now worth taking a moment to ask yourself what you want to get out of this process, as the more you keep your aims and goals in mind, the better chance you will have of making them happen.

So what are you hoping for from this year of exploration? What do you really want? Is there someone you would like to be? If you were living your creativity to the fullest, what do you think your life would look like? And what emotions would you like to feel?

NOW WRITE DOWN WHATEVER COMES TO MIND—YOU CAN ALWAYS COME BACK TO THIS AND ADD NEW IDEAS.

....
....
....
....
....
....
....
....
....
....
....
....

DAY 2

Making a contract

Today is the ideal time to sign up, symbolically, to the commitment you're planning to make over the coming year. Yesterday you noted down what you hope to achieve by reconnecting with your creative self. As you follow this journey, you will need to draw more and more on your inner strengths. So now you're going to make a pledge that you will do everything that's needed to make this work, to be able to live a creative life and enjoy all the benefits that flow from that. To mark this moment, you can actually make a contract with yourself, based on the text below. Then write your own contract on the page opposite. You may find it helpful, over the coming months, to return to this page if you need to boost your motivation.

> *I, ... (name),*
> *Hereby undertake to give myself all the support and encouragement that I can during this journey of discovery aimed at reconnecting with my creative self. I pledge to love, respect, look after, and be kind to myself throughout the year. I will do all I can to bring my talents to life, to believe in myself, and to discover what I love to do, what I can create, and what it means to live a creative life. (sign and date).*

DRAW UP YOUR

CONTRACT

CREATIVITY

How about something a bit more playful?

What do you think about making something that somehow symbolizes what you're doing here with this creative year ahead—an object that is meant just for you and that has special meaning? It can be made of anything—some kind of model, something in paper or cardstock, or sewing, or a piece of jewelry, or a message, or a drawing: something you can carry around with you easily to remind you of the creative journey you have set out on. Close your eyes and imagine this object.

WHAT ARE YOU THINKING ABOUT?

_____

OK, DO YOU HAVE AN IDEA?

Now you can start making it. Obviously, it does not have to be perfect. Work with whatever materials you've got on hand—and if you're mega-inspired, then you can really go to town on this! When you're done, take a picture of what it is that you made, print it out, and stick it in the book.

ATTACH YOUR PHOTO HERE

Keeping a journal

Now it's time to choose a traveling companion for your creative journey. For this, you'll need to go into your favorite craft store or bookstore and pick out the most beautiful notebook you can find. You'll know it when you see it, because it will be like love at first sight: a journal that invites you to open it and write, to add color, to adorn its soft pages and cherish it for the next 365 days.

As the days roll by, you can make it your own, recording everything you're feeling about this creative journey, your emotions, doubts, and discoveries, and adding notes about what you're seeking from a creative life.

CREATED BY YOU, IT WILL BECOME LIKE A TRUSTED FRIEND.

ATTACH A PHOTO OF YOUR NEW NOTEBOOK HERE

Just before you get started...

YOU'LL NEED A SPECIAL BOX!

This will become your very own creative box, a place where you will keep all kinds of inspirational objects and pictures. Ideally, choose a box you find attractive, or get a box and decorate it, perhaps with collage or tape or ribbons or simply a coat of paint.

Call it what you like—perhaps it will become your creative happy box. Most important is what's inside: it could contain a collection of images, or objects or textures, colors, things found in nature or things manufactured, pictures of places and people, perhaps even a ticket stub from an event that you loved, or a scribbled note of a film you saw recently—in short, anything that may have brought a smile to your face. It is a box for beautiful things, strange things, things said and things heard, a paper flower, or simply a piece of beautiful paper.

This box will gradually fill up as the days go on, but you can make a start right now. Keep it handy so it's easy to find. If you think you've run out of inspiration, or you're feeling down, just take a look in the box and get a fix of your little collection of treasures. It will lift your mood—guaranteed!

ATTACH A PHOTO OF
YOUR HAPPY BOX HERE

WHAT WILL YOU START WITH? _____

Making some space

Today's mission is about making a space where you can begin to find your creativity. This will be your creative space, where you can keep your creative happy box, something to write with, and your journal. It needs to be easy to get to, available, and tidy, and will be a place not only to keep your creative stuff, but also where you can sit and think. Once you have found somewhere, you may need to tidy it up a bit, removing anything that you feel is out of step with the person that you are now and who you want to become. Take some time with this task: in a way, it is symbolic of the change you're trying to bring about in your life.

HOW DO YOU FEEL NOW?

Creative visualization

DAY 7

Find yourself a calm and comfortable place where you won't be interrupted.
If you're feeling like it, put on some soft, inspirational music.
Breathe in deeply, and then exhale slowly.

Close your eyes and imagine you can actually see creativity coming down like a great current of energy from the sun, or a divine being, or from the universe itself. Imagine there are rays of light—actually, rays of creativity—coming down and passing right through your body. Feel this energy seeping into every pore. Watch as it nourishes your body, down to the individual cells, which are now glowing with pleasure. You're shining with creativity.
Hold on to the sensation.

HOW DO YOU FEEL NOW?
TRY TO DESCRIBE THE EXPERIENCE. HOW WAS IT?

....
....
....
....
....

Try to hold on to this feeling for the whole day. As the day draws to a close,
how are you feeling? Did you manage to hold on to this feeling?
Did you enjoy the exercise, or did you forget all about it? No need to judge yourself.
But if you liked this exercise, don't hesitate to give it another go…

WRITE DOWN WHAT YOU FELT DURING THE REST OF THE DAY. DID THE FEELING STAY WITH YOU?

....
....
....
....
....
....

THAT'S IT!
WELL DONE FOR
THIS FIRST WEEK!

Now you're all set to start
your year of creativity!

what is creativity?

DAY 8

Time for a definition

Here we are, talking all about creativity, but what does it actually mean?
According to the dictionary, it's about the capacity for invention, imagination, or creative power. Which in turn gives us the capacity to create, imagine, and innovate.

Einstein once described creativity as "intelligence having fun." As for Steve Jobs, he thought that creativity was simply about creating links between things.

We're often talking about creativity in the arts, or in business or in science and technology, but in fact it can be found in every sector of activity and, above all, in our own individual lives. Creativity is something innate in all of us, and we all have it from the moment we are born. But given the paths we take in life, our personal experiences and backgrounds, we can often end up thinking that creativity is not our thing: that we are not creative, or if we are, then only in some kind of limited way.

So let's have a bit of clarity!

WHAT IS YOUR DEFINITION OF CREATIVITY?

....
....
....
....
....
....

WHAT DOES CREATIVITY MEAN FOR YOU, IN YOUR OWN LIFE?

....
....
....
....
....

A bit of research

To carry on with this second week, you'll need to do some detective work to find out where exactly you're starting from when it comes to creativity. So think for a bit about your cultural heritage, about your parents and upbringing, and what you have taken from all these aspects and whether it suits you … or not! Answer as honestly as you can, and take your time. The main thing is to think about the questions. Answers will emerge eventually, perhaps hours or even days later.

WHY ARE YOU INTERESTED IN CREATIVITY IN THE FIRST PLACE?

What do you think creativity can deliver for you? What's your aim in becoming more creative? What fundamental change do you think you will be able to make to your life, in your behavior, as a result of creativity? And how is that important to you?

....
....
....
....
....
....
....

DO YOU THINK YOU'RE NOT CREATIVE ENOUGH? WHY IS THAT? AND HOW DOES IT PLAY OUT IN YOUR LIFE?

....
....
....
....
....
....
....
....
....
....
....
....

Continuing our investigation …

HOW DO YOUR PARENTS, FAMILY, AND FRIENDS VIEW CREATIVITY?

....
....
....
....

HOW DID THEY VIEW YOUR CREATIVITY WHEN YOU WERE A CHILD? DID THEY ENCOURAGE YOU?

....
....
....
....

AND HOW DID YOU EXPERIENCE YOUR OWN CREATIVITY IN YOUR CHILDHOOD?

....
....
....

HOW DID YOUR PARENTS LIVE OUT THEIR CREATIVITY?

....
....
....

DOES ANY OF THIS EXPLAIN YOUR CURRENT BELIEFS ABOUT CREATIVITY?

....
....
....
....

WHAT KIND OF CREATIVE THINGS DID YOU DO AS A CHILD?

....
....
....
....

WHAT DID YOUR PARENTS SAY OR THINK ABOUT ARTISTIC PEOPLE? CAN YOU RECALL THEIR VIEWS?

• Artists are …

....

• Musicians are …

....

• Painters are …

....

HOW DID THEY VIEW THE ARTISTIC WORLD? WHAT DID THEY TEACH YOU ABOUT THE WORLD OF CREATIVE PEOPLE?

....
....
....
....
....

WHAT DID YOU THINK ABOUT YOUR PARENTS' BELIEFS?

....
....
....
....

AND HOW ABOUT NOW? DO YOU NOW THINK THE SAME THING AS YOUR PARENTS?

....
....
....
....
....
....
....
....
....
....

Going a little further

WHO ARE YOUR CREATIVE HEROES?
You may not know them personally, but can you name five people that you think are really creative?

....
....

WHAT ASPECT OF THEM MAKES THEM SO CREATIVE?

....
....
....

HOW DO YOU THINK A REALLY CREATIVE PERSON SHOULD BEHAVE?

....
....
....

WHAT ARE THE STAND-OUT QUALITIES, DO YOU THINK, IN SOMEONE CREATIVE?

....
....
....

DO YOU HAVE SOME OF THESE QUALITIES?

....
....
....

AND WHAT DO YOU THINK ARE SOME TYPICAL DRAWBACKS IN CREATIVE PEOPLE?

....
....
....
....

Some final questions

HAVE YOU EVER BEEN TOLD THAT CREATIVITY IS RESERVED FOR "ARTISTS"—FOR A CREATIVE ELITE?

....
....
....
....

DO YOU TEND TO PUT "CREATIVITY" ON A PEDESTAL?

....
....

DO YOU THINK CREATIVE PEOPLE HAVE A PLACE IN SOCIETY? WHY? WHAT SORT OF PEOPLE?

....
....
....
....

DO YOU THINK CREATIVITY IS AN INNATE GIFT AMONG CERTAIN PEOPLE?

....
....
....

DO YOU THINK CREATIVITY CAN BE ENCOURAGED TO DEVELOP? (IF YOU'RE READING THIS BOOK, YOU PROBABLY DO!)

....
....
....

BY CREATING, WE BECOME CREATIVE. BY PRACTICING, WE GET BETTER. HOW DOES THAT MAKE YOU FEEL?

....
....
....
....

Time to see what we've got going on

SO AFTER ALL THIS BRAINSTORMING, HAS ANYTHING COME UP? HOW ARE YOU FEELING NOW?

....
....
....
....
....

HAVE THE QUESTIONS FROM THE PREVIOUS DAYS RAISED ANY FURTHER QUESTIONS? IF SO, WRITE THEM HERE:

....
....
....
....
....

HAVE YOU SPOTTED CERTAIN INGRAINED PATTERNS IN YOUR WAY OF THINKING? HAVE YOU CHALLENGED SOME OF THESE IDEAS?

....
....
....
....
....

Ready to fly?

After this quick overview, you're now going to embrace your life with a big YES! Say yes to creativity, yes to change. No more putting creativity on a pedestal. It is simple, not sophisticated. And it's time to live, and time to create!

On the page opposite, write a huge YES in your favorite color. Then take some felt-tip pens and draw on your "creative wings." If you prefer to make some wings—using fabric, or paper, or feathers—then don't hold back!

Close your eyes and take a deep breath. Imagine your creative wings are starting to grow. Feel them slowly expanding and unfolding. Try to follow every sensation, and when you feel ready, imagine your wings beating, lifting you up, and carrying you weightlessly along the path of creativity.

Reconnect
– with your inner child

DAY 15

Reconnection

THIS WEEK, HOW ABOUT RECONNECTING WITH YOUR INNER CHILD?

They are in there somewhere, you as a small child, fascinated by everything, at times almost bursting with spontaneous joy. Your "inner child" holds the keys to your creativity, unlocking a time when everything seemed simple, playful, and fun. If you can connect with that small person that you used to be, then you may find yourself tapping into some amazing inner strengths.

Close your eyes and relax. Picture your inner child, having a wonderful time, happy and playful. Now think back in time from where you are right now, working back through the layers of your life, back to the point (however long ago) where you can feel pretty certain that you were a child who loved to play, or draw, color, invent things, or just sing your heart out.

Now visualize yourself at that age, this joyful, freewheeling kid who marvels at the world around them. At that moment, you were perfectly connected with your creative spirit.

WHAT ARE YOU FEELING NOW? CAN YOU DESCRIBE IT?

....
....
....
....
....

If you find you cannot connect with your inner child, or if you feel that this is a painful experience that is making you unhappy, then best to leave this exercise alone. Perhaps you might also consider talking to a trusted specialist about some of the feelings that this brought up. Trying to reconcile your adult self with aspects of a difficult childhood experience is hard, and best done with professional help.

Let's start a dialogue

DAY 16

Shut your eyes and breathe deeply. Imagine your inner child. Where are they? Start a conversation with them. Give them a hug. Explain that you're starting this journey of discovery, and you want them to come along with you. Listen patiently and kindly to their reactions. Will they join you? Maybe you need to encourage them a little, but the main thing is to start that conversation.

You could do the same exercise again, this time with the help of a photograph of yourself when you were a child. Look closely at the photograph and really try to connect, heart to heart, with that child. Send them your love. And then, stick the photo into this book. If you don't have a photograph, do a drawing, as a kid would do, using markers or colored pencils. When you feel you need to reconnect with that inner child, just take another look at the picture.

HOW DID THAT GO?

....
....
....
....
....
....
....
....
....
....
....
....
....

Make their wish come true

Spending time with your inner child will help you reinforce a sense of self-love and, with this feeling of being loved and supported, you may feel much more easily a sense of that childlike energy coming back to you. And a sense of being reconciled with yourself.

CLOSE YOUR EYES AND VISUALIZE YOUR INNER CHILD. HOW ARE THEY DOING?

Ask them if they'd like to do something special with you. What will it be? A tickling match? Singing and dancing? Having an ice cream? Jumping into some puddles?

Ask if they want to do some drawing or coloring, or build a fort, or run, jump, and dance—however they want to express their creativity, which for them seems so effortless. Find out what they like to do, and now try to do that, whatever it is, this very day.

HOW ARE YOU FEELING NOW?

....
....
....
....
....
....
....
....
....

ATTACH A PHOTO OF
THAT MOMENT

Child's play

DO YOU REMEMBER THE GAMES YOU PLAYED AS A KID?

What were they? What did you particularly like to play? Why? How are you feeling now?
Do you manage to recapture the joy of these games? Take your time to allow some
memories to return, and write here what comes up.

....
....
....
....
....
....
....

Take a moment to play one of your favorite games or pastimes. It could be dressing up,
or coloring, or playing ball. Whatever it is, try to experience it as your inner child would have.
Have as much fun as you possibly can, of course!

If you can, take a photo.

ATTACH THE PHOTO OF
YOU PLAYING

Creative shopping

This time, you're going to bring your inner child on a shopping trip to a craft store. Have fun testing out the markers, glitter pens, the whole lot! Let your inner child inspire you to choose what would make them happy while they join you on your journey.

WHAT DO THEY LIKE? CHOOSE WHAT IS GOING TO MAKE YOU BOTH HAPPY: STICKERS, TAPE, PAPER—ALL USEFUL IN THE CREATIVE PROCESS. DESCRIBE YOUR EXPERIENCE HERE.

....
....
....
....
....
....
....
....
....
....
....
....
....
....
....
....

A meet-up with your inner artist

Here is an exercise from the marvelous book by Julia Cameron, *The Artist's Way*. You're going to meet up with your "inner artist." All you need to do is go on an outing with this inner-child-artist, which can put some creative magic into your life.

BREATHE IN, AND FOCUS ON YOUR INNER CHILD. SHUT YOUR EYES, AND VISUALIZE YOUR INNER ARTIST. HOW ARE THEY DOING? ASK WHAT ACTIVITY THEY'D LIKE TO DO WITH YOU.

WRITE DOWN THE ANSWERS HERE.

....
....
....
....
....
....
....
....

NOW TAKE YOUR DIARY AND MAKE A TIME OVER THE COMING WEEK TO ENACT ONE OF THEIR IDEAS.

ON THE DAY, GIVE UP TIME JUST TO MAKE YOUR INNER CHILD HAPPY ENCOURAGING THEIR CREATIVITY AND JOY, SHOWING THEM YOUR SUPPORT, AND IN TURN ENJOYING THEIR PARTICIPATION IN YOUR CREATIVITY!

Time for something special

Today, you're going to give a beautiful present to your inner child. First, think about them, get in touch, and ask what kind of present they would love to receive. Ask them if they'd like a toy—and what kind? A doll, or maybe a fire truck. Then suggest to them that you make one, the two of you, together. With your inner child firmly in mind, get hold of all the stuff you're going to need to create this present, and then start to make it. It may take some time, but do it with a joyful heart. If you like, take a photo of what you have made, and stick it into this book.

HOW DO YOU FEEL NOW? IMAGINE GIVING THIS TO YOUR INNER CHILD. WHAT IS THEIR REACTION?

....
....
....
....
....

ATTACH THE PHOTO OF YOUR PRESENT HERE

Permission to create!

DAY 22

It's your right ...

DO YOU ACTUALLY ALLOW YOURSELF THE RIGHT TO LIVE A CREATIVE LIFE?

Do you let yourself be creative in all aspects of your life—as creative as you'd really like to be? If not, what do you think is holding you back? Are you waiting for someone to give you "permission"? Maybe your friends, family, parents, or perhaps just one individual?

Are you letting other people be the gatekeepers of your creativity? Is it because you don't want to get in their way? How do you feel about this situation? Take some time to reflect a little on the emotions that come up as you think about this ...

....
....
....
....
....
....
....
....
....
....
....
....
....
....
....
....
....
....
....
....

What if?

WHAT IF YOU REALLY ALLOWED YOURSELF TO BE CREATIVE?

If you had permission, approval, or encouragement from everyone you know, whether or not they are still alive, or indeed some form of celestial permission from the entire universe, from the whole of creation: what would you like to create? Take a moment to imagine how it would be to live your creativity to the fullest. Describe what your life would be like: how does it feel?

....
....
....
....
....
....
....
....
....
....
....
....
....
....
....
....
....
....
....
....
....
....
....

As life draws to a close...

Imagine you're at the very end of your life, on the threshold of the next world, and you take a look back at the life you have lived. What would you like to be able to feel at this point? The sense of having lived life to the fullest? Are you proud of what you have done? Or maybe you have regrets for the things that you didn't achieve?

WHAT WOULD YOU LIKE TO HAVE CREATED?

DAY 24

Would you feel you had done everything in your power to make your dreams become reality? Take a moment to think about the questions above, and write your answers here.

....
....
....
....
....
....
....
....
....
....
....
....
....
....
....
....
....
....
....
....
....
....
....
....
....

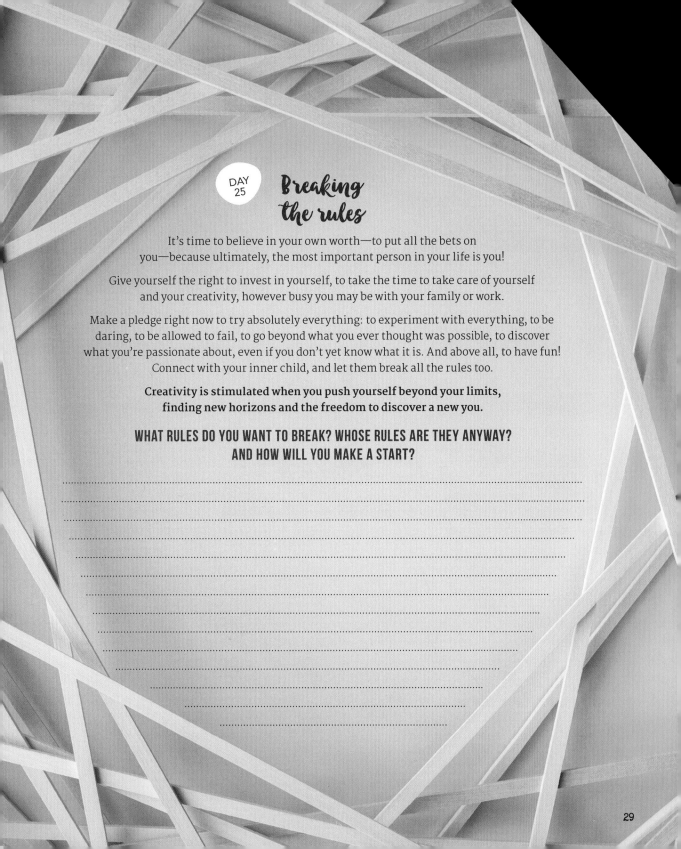

DAY 25

Breaking the rules

It's time to believe in your own worth—to put all the bets on you—because ultimately, the most important person in your life is you!

Give yourself the right to invest in yourself, to take the time to take care of yourself and your creativity, however busy you may be with your family or work.

Make a pledge right now to try absolutely everything: to experiment with everything, to be daring, to be allowed to fail, to go beyond what you ever thought was possible, to discover what you're passionate about, even if you don't yet know what it is. And above all, to have fun! Connect with your inner child, and let them break all the rules too.

Creativity is stimulated when you push yourself beyond your limits, finding new horizons and the freedom to discover a new you.

WHAT RULES DO YOU WANT TO BREAK? WHOSE RULES ARE THEY ANYWAY? AND HOW WILL YOU MAKE A START?

....
....
....
....
....
....
....
....
....
....
....
....

...cense

...paints, your creative happy box, ...p, and now you can make your ...Creative License! The idea here is to have as much fun as possible, to get totally engrossed in the project. Stick a photo on when you're done.

YOUR TEXT COULD BE SOMETHING LIKE THIS:

> I, ... (name),
> hereby grant myself permission to live out my creativity to the fullest in every single aspect of my life, for the greatest benefit both to myself and to all of those around me.
> (sign and date)

ATTACH YOUR CREATIVE LICENSE HERE!

CHOOSE SOMEWHERE IN YOUR HOUSE TO DISPLAY YOUR CREATIVE LICENSE, SO YOU CAN LOOK AT IT EVERY DAY AND BE INSPIRED!

Bonus day

With the whole week spent thinking about "permission," today is going to be your special bonus day where you have permission to do (or not do) whatever you want!

HOW WAS IT? HOW DID THE DAY GO, AND HOW DID YOU FEEL?

....
....
....
....
....
....
....
....
....
....
....

DAY 28

Congratulations!

You deserve to be proud of yourself! You have just completed the first four weeks of your new creative life. How are you feeling so far? How did these weeks go? What have been the hardest parts? Look back over your notes, and see how far you've come.

HOW WILL YOU CELEBRATE THIS SPECIAL DAY?

Starting from
- where you are -

DAY 29

Where are you in your creative journey?

This week, I'd like to invite you to accept where you are creatively. The first thing to do is to fully accept your current situation. It may not be exactly where you want to be, and it may not reflect many of your hopes and desires. But it is only by accepting yourself as you are now that you will start to be able to tap into your very own creative powers.

WHERE DO YOU THINK YOU ARE TODAY, IN TERMS OF YOUR CREATIVITY? DO YOU FEEL LIKE A TOTAL BEGINNER, OR LIKE SOMEONE WITH SOME EXPERTISE IN THIS AREA?

....
....
....
....
....
....
....
....
....
....
....
....
....
....
....

CREATIVITY ACROSS YOUR WHOLE LIFE?

Think about the various aspects of your life that are listed in the table, and then, on a scale of 1 to 10, score each one in terms of how creative you feel you are. Are you feeling more creative, or less creative, than, say, a couple of years ago? You can indicate this with an arrow up, down, or flat, next to the score.

	↗ ↘ SCORE
HEALTH	
FAMILY	
WORK	
FINANCE	
INTIMATE RELATIONSHIPS	
SEXUALITY	
FRIENDSHIP	
SOCIAL INTERACTIONS	
SPIRITUALITY	
WELL-BEING	

Some conclusions

TAKE ANOTHER LOOK AT THAT TABLE YOU FILLED IN. DO YOU NOTICE ANY PARTICULAR TRENDS?

And in which areas of your life in particular? Can you identify which parts of your life seem to be the most creative? How do you experience that?

Where you are right now may not be close to where you want to get to. But how about accepting where you are now, while still holding on strongly to your ultimate dreams and desires?

....
....
....
....
....
....
....
....
....
....
....

What do you think is the biggest difficulty that you're facing in trying to let your creativity emerge more fully? How well (or not) are you coping with that? And what kind of problem is it?

WHAT WILL IT TAKE FOR YOU TO BE ABLE TO LIVE MORE CREATIVELY?

....
....
....
....
....
....
....
....
....
....
....
....
....

Your values

The values you hold will underpin every aspect of your creativity. So being clear about what these are will help you engage much more deeply with your creative endeavors. If you want to really get into the kind of creativity that you're dreaming of, being aware of these values will help take you there.

What are your values in terms of creativity? And among the other values in your life, where would you place creativity?

A FEW IDEAS :
JOY, GENEROSITY, ORIGINALITY, FREEDOM

MAKE A LIST

In the space below, draw a large sun using markers.
In its center, write "creativity." On each of the sun's rays, write one of your values—and any others that come to mind.

HOW DOES THIS MAKE YOU FEEL?

DAY
32

Some other scenarios

Look again at what you wrote in the table on Day 29, and pick one of the aspects of your life where you would like to boost your creativity. How do you feel you could be more creative? Think of three different scenarios that would allow you to stimulate your creativity.

WRITE ABOUT THEM HERE.

....
....
....
....
....
....
....
....
....
....

DAY
33

What really inspires you?

Do you know what you're really passionate about in your life? It needn't be something directly linked with creativity. But reconnecting with what you love to do brings you energy and dynamism, and is high-octane fuel for your creativity!

What really inspires you? To the point where you're getting up in the middle of the night to write down an idea in a notepad? What are the subjects that make you so absorbed you lose all track of time, where it's all about the joy of the moment?

WRITE DOWN WHAT REALLY INSPIRES YOU AND WHY YOU'RE SO PASSIONATE ABOUT IT.

....
....
....
....
....
....
....
....
....

What do you like?

UNDERSTANDING WHAT YOU LIKE, AND WHERE YOUR INTERESTS LIE, IS AN IMPORTANT STARTING POINT. WHAT DO YOU LIKE TO DO? MAKE A LIST.

This list will be a kind of "database" of your likes and tastes. After all, what you create will of course have a link with who you are, and with what you like (or dislike) in life. If you're not really sure what it is you like in life, then it's time to ask yourself this question. You can keep coming back to this list, and complete it as the weeks go on.

What do you like in terms of music, art, books, cooking, travel, science, culture, or sport? Are there past civilizations that you feel drawn to, and why? Who are your creative heroes and heroines?

....
....
....
....
....
....
....
....
....
....
....
....
....
....
....
....
....
....
....
....
....
....
....
....

Creative workshop

In the space below, draw a tree. On each of the main branches of the tree, write in the activities you love to do. Use the ideas that came up yesterday, and write in everything to do with your passions and interests on the smaller branches and the leaves.

You can even write your values from Day 31 in the trunk.

Your dreams!

DAY 36

Childhood dreams

Rediscovering your childhood aspirations can help you to reconnect with your deepest desires and motivations, in their pure state—before society and your surroundings began to put the brakes on things. Close your eyes and imagine the child you used to be.

BREATHE IN DEEPLY, AND ASK THEM ABOUT THEIR HOPES AND DREAMS. WHAT OR WHO DID THEY HOPE TO BECOME?

What were they passionate about? Be patient, because the answers may not come to you straight away. Note down any thoughts you have, and watch during the day for anything that links back to this question.

....
....
....
....
....
....
....
....
....
....
....
....
....
....
....
....
....

Teen ambitions

Let's do the same exercise as yesterday, but this time with the teen that you used to be. Close your eyes and try to visualize that time in your life. It may help to look at a photograph of yourself from that time as you do so.

BREATHE IN DEEPLY AND ASK THEM ABOUT THEIR HOPES, PLANS, AND AMBITIONS.

As you did yesterday, write down the ideas that come to mind, without adding in any kind of filter or judgment. Be patient, and complete this list later if more ideas come to mind.

....
....
....
....
....
....
....
....
....
....
....
....
....
....
....
....
....
....
....
....
....
....
....
....
....
....
....

What did you want to be?

IF ANYTHING WAS POSSIBLE, WHAT JOB WOULD YOU HAVE DREAMED OF DOING?

What jobs attracted you when you were younger? What did you dream of doing, and is there anything left of that dream in your life at the moment? How could you pick up some of those dreams where you left them back then, and maybe breathe new life into them?

Make a list of anything that comes to mind, and make a date in your diary to take a first step toward reconnecting with one of those early dreams or ambitions. Which will it be?

....
....
....
....
....
....
....
....
....
....
....
....
....
....
....
....
....
....
....
....
....
....
....
....
....
....

Now for your craziest ideas

To take this just a bit further, try to remember your craziest, most secret ambitions from your youth. Obviously, this will not be easy, and may take some time to recall, but be patient with yourself, and start excavating the past! Don't stop when you remember just one thing—it could reveal a bunch of other forgotten ideas, too!

WHAT WERE YOUR CRAZIEST AMBITIONS? DID YOU ACHIEVE ANY OF THEM? DO THEY FORM EVEN A SMALL PART OF YOUR LIFE TODAY?

....
....
....
....
....
....
....
....
....
....
....
....
....
....

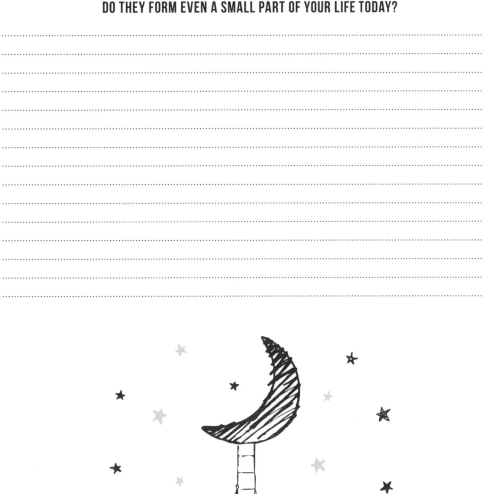

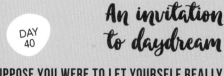

An invitation to daydream

SUPPOSE YOU WERE TO LET YOURSELF REALLY DREAM AND TO ALLOW YOURSELF DREAMS THAT GO WAY BEYOND THE POSSIBLE: WHAT WOULD THAT BE LIKE?

Lie down on your bed or on the couch, with some soft music playing in the background. Let your thoughts float freely, as if carried up on the wings of your own imagination toward a magical world full of breathtaking landscapes. Now, imagine you're embarking on a voyage on a wonderful ship, which is going to take you to a place where all your biggest dreams will come true. Where would that be? What would that voyage be like?

And what if you had a magic wand? If time and money were no object, what would you dream of doing? Dive with whales in the Antarctic? Travel in the blink of an eye to a distant star? It's time to set your imagination free!

HOW ARE YOU FEELING NOW?

....
....
....
....
....
....
....
....
....
....
....

Creative workshop

Now's the time to make your own magic wand, one that will give you special powers in making those dreams come true. Begin by sketching out how you'd like it to be, what it looks like, how it might be decorated. Does it have feathers, or maybe ribbons? Or pearls, or shells? Will you paint a design on it? Now go out and find everything you need to bring it into reality.

TAKE A MOMENT TO PLAN HOW YOU'LL MAKE IT. WHEN IT'S DONE, TAKE A PICTURE, PRINT IT, AND ATTACH IT HERE.

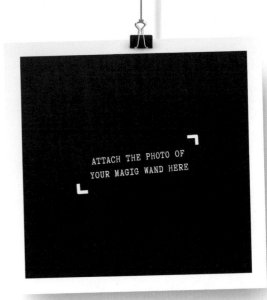

ATTACH THE PHOTO OF YOUR MAGIC WAND HERE

Who do you want to be?

Imagine you're approaching the end of your days, having led a life that has been happy, creative, and full. Write down what you'd like to say to younger members of your family about the kinds of hopes and dreams they too might be able to make reality one day.

WHAT WOULD YOU LIKE TO TELL THEM?

....
....
....
....
....
....
....
....

You're
- worth it! -

Can you recognize your own worth?

How can you figure out your own value? Not just your value in a creative sense, but the qualities in you that help build up your sense of who you are: your self-confidence, pure and simple.

Maybe it is tricky to work this one out, to get this sense of personal value, and your creative value. Why do you think this is? What are the qualities that you can identify? Can you see any specific ones?

What are your skills, your knowledge, your personal qualities? What kind of things do you find easy to do, a breeze to understand?

START MAKING A LIST, WHICH YOU CAN ADD TO AS TIME GOES ON.

....
....
....
....
....
....
....
....
....
....
....
....

Your focus

You are who you are, and that, in itself, is quite enough, and what's more, it's actually great! So all the stuff about value does not mean we need to ignore our "faults." But if you're too hard on yourself and as a result can't recognize your own unique value, this will sabotage your creativity. If you focus on what you think you're lacking, you will believe it even more strongly.

Do you know the story of the two wolves, living inside a man, fighting for survival? There is a good wolf and a bad wolf. Which one will win?

ANSWER: the one you feed!

WHAT DOES THIS STORY MAKE YOU THINK ABOUT? HOW ABOUT YOU SPEND YOUR DAY "FEEDING THE GOOD WOLF"?

....
....
....
....
....

AND HOW ABOUT YOUR "FAULTS"? WHAT ARE THEY? WHAT DON'T YOU LIKE?

Choose five, and then see how there is also something good hidden in each of these faults.

For example, if you think you talk too much, it also shows a strong desire to communicate with others. If you're stubborn, it is also a quality of exaggerated perseverance.

Note down your "faults" and the quality hidden within each.

....
....
....
....
....
....
....
....

Are you letting others determine your worth?

Don't wait for others to talk up your creative worth before heading out on your own creative adventure. Because it may never happen. When it comes to this particular creative enterprise, you're your own boss. So don't let anyone make you think that you're not up to it. And don't let your own inner voice do so either.

DO YOU LET OTHER PEOPLE JUDGE YOUR CREATIVE WORTH?

What does this phrase make you think? Does it evoke anything specific? Have you experienced this kind of judgment before? If so, when? How would you choose to react if it happened now?

....
....
....
....
....
....
....
....
....
....
....
....
....
....
....
....
....
....
....

Here's the antidote to all that negativity: think of the five things you have done that you're most proud of, no matter if they're creative or not. Describe them below, and savor the energy and dynamism of those moments.

HOW ARE YOU FEELING NOW?

....
....
....
....
....
....
....
....
....
....
....
....
....
....

It's complimentary

How do you react when you receive a compliment? Do you tend to say, "No, really, it's nothing …"?

HOW EASILY DO YOU TAKE A COMPLIMENT?

....
....
....
....
....
....
....

(continued on next page)

Now, how about getting a small notebook and writing in (using as many colors as you like) the kind of spontaneous compliments that you might receive: all those encouraging little words and gestures.

Over the coming weeks and months, collect up all these compliments, writing them in the notebook when they happen. Keep this notebook handy, and when you feel a bit fed up or worn down, take a look at all these compliments and feel your energy level surge!

....
....
....
....
....
....
....
....
....
....
....
....
....

HOW COULD YOU IMPROVE YOUR SENSE OF YOUR OWN PERSONAL VALUE?

....
....
....
....
....
....
....
....
....
....
....
....
....
....

Three great qualities

Christine Lewicky, in her book *Wake Up*, suggests asking your five closest friends to tell you what your three most important qualities are, and in what situations you have shown these in your life. I'd like to ask you to do that today. Who will you ask?

Note down the responses in the space below. How far does this resonate with your own ideas of who you are? It can be a surprising exercise, as our friends often seem to know us even better than we know ourselves!

WHAT WAS THE EXPERIENCE LIKE FOR YOU?

....
....
....
....
....
....
....
....
....
....
....
....
....
....
....
....
....
....
....
....
....
....
....

Give yourself some credit

Do you give yourself the credit you deserve? Don't just wait for everyone else to say nice things, as this can hold up your creative energy and leave you "on hold." Do you find yourself waiting for approval or recognition from someone in your life? If so, who is it?

....

....

....

....

....

WHAT DO YOU BELIEVE YOU DESERVE?

Make a list, inspired by the following text if you like.

> *You, (your name)*
> *You deserve to succeed. You deserve to be creative. You deserve to be loved, and to be fully and richly creative. You deserve to be happy. I am proud of you, and it is really amazing what you're doing, putting your time into this creative journey.*

YOU,

....

....

....

....

....

....

....

....

....

....

....

....

....

....

....

Now, stand in front of a mirror, look yourself in the eyes, and tell yourself, out loud, all the things that you deserve.

HOW WAS THIS EXERCISE FOR YOU? HOW DO YOU FEEL NOW?

....

....

....

....

....

....

....

....

....

....

Congratulations!

Get into the habit of giving yourself a pat on the back from time to time, recognizing those small victories—or major achievements, when you have dared to take a big step forward—launching your first blog, taking some photos, making a video, or maybe even knitting your first ever sweater? Wow!
Bravo! You can be proud of yourself.

WHAT WOULD YOU LIKE TO GIVE YOURSELF TO MARK THIS SPECIAL MOMENT? FLOWERS, A GIFT, SOME ME-TIME, OR MAYBE A MASSAGE?

WRITE DOWN WHAT COMES TO MIND.

....
....
....
....
....
....
....
....
....
....
....
....
....
....

. WEEK 8 .
the creative process

The essential stages

Having a clear idea of the creative process is a major benefit when it comes to getting projects off the ground. The cycle of stages shown below will provide you with a kind of compass to work out where you are and what to expect. It may also help you to get going if you hit a creative block. Described by Clarissa Pinkola Estés and completed by Anne-Marie Jobin*, this creative process is a "journey between two worlds, the spiritual and the material."
I love this description.

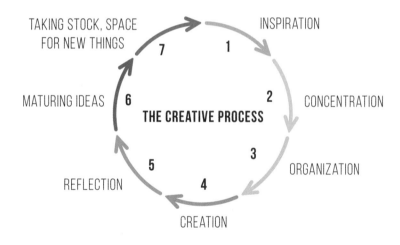

TAKING STOCK, SPACE FOR NEW THINGS — 7
INSPIRATION — 1
MATURING IDEAS — 6
CONCENTRATION — 2
THE CREATIVE PROCESS
REFLECTION — 5
ORGANIZATION — 3
CREATION — 4

DOES THIS DIAGRAM RESONATE WITH YOU? DO YOU SEE ANY PARALLELS WITH THE CREATIVE PROCESS THAT YOU EXPERIENCE OR HAVE SEEN? WHAT IS YOUR CREATIVE PROCESS LIKE? WRITE DOWN YOUR THOUGHTS.

....
....
....
....
....
....
....

* Anne-Marie Jobin : Créez la Vie Qui Vous Ressemble

Stage 1:
Defining your intentions →

Some people feel a deep desire to create something, but never manage to catch the thread of inspiration. There's too much confusion of thoughts to be able to arrive at a viable creative project. So we need to take a step back, to make a space where inspiration can come in, taking time to redefine what it is that motivates and inspires us. Try to look into your own self, and question your motivation—which can in turn add clarity to your vision. It is really worthwhile asking the "why" question about your project, which will keep you from running out of gas half way through the creation. If you're feeling a bit take-it-or-leave-it about your project, then change something: either your goal is not properly defined, or the way you're going about it is not working for you, or maybe it is simply not "your" project at all.

DO YOU HAVE A PROJECT THAT IS CLOSE TO YOUR HEART? TRY TO DEFINE WHAT THIS IS ABOUT.

What are you really hoping for? Why is this project important to you? What does it inspire in you? What do you like about it? Why do you feel so passionately about it?

....
....
....
....
....
....
....
....
....

Draw a shooting star, like in the sketch below. At the center of the star, write your main objective to guide you through the process. On the rays of the star, write what inspires you about it. And on the trail behind the star, write the stages you will go through to complete it.

Stage 2: Inspiration

This is the exciting phase where you start to feel a strong, almost intuitive pull toward a certain idea. You let yourself be carried by the flow of ideas and imagination, where anything seems possible. You set out from a certain starting point and begin to visualize how this could look. You are in creative overdrive! This is an ideal time to keep a notebook close by, and jot down anything that comes into your head, because all your ideas are finding fertile ground.

HAVE YOU EXPERIENCED THIS PHASE DURING YOUR CREATIVE LIFE?

Do you remember a time like this in your life? In your current project, have you been able to open the floodgates of your imagination? Do you allow yourself to dream big about your project and bring in all your ideas? What kinds of ideas are they?

....
....
....
....
....
....
....
....

Stage 3: Concentration of energy

After the inspiration phase, the energy levels change somewhat and you need to slow things down and focus on getting the project underway. So many projects never get beyond the inspiration phase because the process of concentration takes effort and is a lot less fun. It's the time to make big choices, sort out the ideas that you need and those you don't, and begin to set some priorities.

HOW WILL YOU BE ABLE TO BRING THIS KIND OF FOCUS TO YOUR CURRENT PROJECT? START TO SORT OUT YOUR IDEAS, AND WRITE DOWN WHAT YOUR PRIORITIES NEED TO BE.

....
....
....
....
....
....
....
....
....
....
....
....
....

Stage 4: Organization

This is all about figuring out what will be the main stages of your project as precisely as possible, so you have a "road map" of what needs to be done. Of course, there's a whole bunch of guesswork involved because you don't know exactly how things will turn out, but having this kind of planning in place will really help you achieve what you want.

START BY DIVIDING YOUR PROJECT INTO ITS MAIN STAGES. THEN, THINK ABOUT THE SMALLER STEPS REQUIRED TO ACHIEVE EACH OF THESE STAGES.

Try to plan how much time will be needed for each stage, and perhaps even fix a precise date for achieving an important part of the project. For example, if you're researching new ideas, you could give yourself three weeks to explore three different areas. Write down your objective, the next stage that will be required, and how long you'll give yourself to achieve it.

....
....
....
....
....
....
....
....
....
....
....
....
....
....
....
....
....
....
....

Stage 5: Creation

You've done the planning, and it's time to make something happen. But take your time. If you have been following the previous stages carefully and thoughtfully, it will be easy enough to get started on the making part of the project. Get your workspace set up so everything is ready, and get stuck in! As Goethe wrote: "Begin, and the work is done."

Of course, in this practical stage, all that creative thinking will come head-to-head with the physical world of actually doing, and you can expect plenty of unforeseen difficulties. This is where your skills will be tested, along with your ability to come up with original solutions..

....
....
....
....
....
....
....
....
....
....
....
....
....
....
....
....
....
....
....
....
....
....
....
....

Stage 6: Thinking and follow-up

The creating stage is complete, but there is an important stage that comes right afterward that is all about reflecting on what you have created and somehow "coming down" from the creative high. It is a moment to take stock of the work you have done, think about what you have learned from the creative experience, and see what pitfalls you might be able to avoid in the future.

This step allows you to appreciate what you have accomplished, and to give yourself a pat on the back: even if the finished project may not seem "perfect," it has at least seen the light of day. Take a look at how you made it happen.

HOW WOULD YOU ASSESS ONE OF YOUR OWN CREATIVE PROJECTS?
WHAT NEEDS TO IMPROVE, AND WHAT ASPECTS ARE YOU MOST PROUD OF?
HOW WOULD YOU CELEBRATE FINISHING THIS PROJECT?

....
....
....
....
....
....
....
....
....
....
....
....
....
....
....
....
....
....
....
....
....
....

Creative
– warm-ups –

Finding inspiration

It's not always easy to plunge yourself into a frenzy of creativity at the click of your fingers. So this week we're looking at a series of **creative warm-ups** that will help get you in the creating mood. Just like stretching out before a run, these will help you get more easily into a creative groove, and also overcome some of those mental blockages that so often get in the way.

The exercises that follow will encourage you to develop a kind of preparatory stage—unique to you—that will help you get into a creative frame of mind. It could also become a welcome daily ritual. See what you think.

SO LET'S GET STARTED AND CREATE YOUR OWN WARM-UP RITUAL.

Take a few minutes to think about how you could create this kind of ritual: How would you like to start? A short meditation, perhaps? A candle, or some incense? Maybe it's drawing or coloring. The main thing is that this moment feels nourishing, and it makes you feel good.

Write down what you like

Here's an exercise to do in the mornings if you feel that you are a bit short on motivation. Write down 20 things that you like. No need to think hard, just write 'em down! Things you love to do—simple, easy things, like listening to a song. Then read them out loud to yourself, thinking why you like each of these so much.

HOW DO YOU FEEL NOW? HAVE YOU FELT THINGS SHIFTING?

If that's not enough, then start over, and carry on until you feel ready for some creative action.

....

....

....

....

....

....

....

In touch with your feelings

This time, write down how you would like to spend an ideal day, or how you would like to experience a moment of creativity, and what you would hope to feel.

WRITE DOWN YOUR THOUGHTS AND IDEAS HERE.

....

....

....

....

....

....

....

....

....

....

....

....

....

A creative "To Do" list

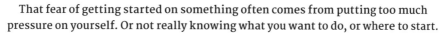

That fear of getting started on something often comes from putting too much pressure on yourself. Or not really knowing what you want to do, or where to start.

TAKE TIME TO REVIEW WHAT YOU DID YESTERDAY. WHERE ARE YOU NOW IN YOUR PROJECT?

....
....
....
....
....
....

We may all hate the dreaded "To Do" list, but one thing it does is help define what you need to do in the coming week, and establish a sense of priority. Here's how: take a sheet of paper and note down the days of the week, and then divide up what you need to do across the various days. Feel free to make it look pretty! Think about tiny tasks as well as the big stuff, and don't put too much pressure on yourself to get it all done in the right order. Pick out one of the tasks, depending on how you're feeling, and enjoy the immense pleasure of crossing out the task when it's done. Whenever you feel the need, there's nothing to stop you from making a new list later in the week.

WHAT DO YOU THINK? ARE YOU READY FOR YOUR "TO DO" LIST?

....
....
....
....
....
....

The inspired pencil

Starting from the point of the pencil drawn at the bottom of this page, write whatever you want, in any direction on the page, anything at all, with no grammar required. Just write down whatever comes into your head!

HOW DO YOU FEEL NOW?

....
....
....
....
....

START YOUR WRITING
HERE

DAY
62

All over the place

Find an inspiring image from your creative happy box, stick it onto a sheet of paper, and write down what you find inspirational about it, turning the sheet of paper from time to time as you go, so that your writing goes all over the place and in all directions.

HOW DO YOU FEEL NOW?

....
....
....
....
....
....
....
....
....
....
....
....

ATTACH A PHOTO OF
YOUR CREATION HERE!

The why question

Sometimes, the best way to get a project back on track is to remember why you're doing it.

WHY DOES YOUR PROJECT INSPIRE YOU? WHY DID YOU CHOOSE IT? AND WHAT DO YOU LIKE MOST ABOUT IT?

Take the first idea that comes to mind and write it down—and then the next. Don't think too hard, just write them down. Try to put some meaning back into your project.

HOW DO YOU FEEL?

WEEK 10
The creative toolbox

This week, we'll be looking at some techniques that could help you along the way to rediscovering your creativity. It's mix 'n match: just choose what you feel will be helpful.

DAY 64

Spontaneous writing: morning pages

Here is an exercise from Julia Cameron's excellent book *The Artist's Way*. What she calls **morning pages** are three sheets of longhand, stream-of-consciousness writing you do each morning. It's a bit like a private journal, with the content meant for your eyes only, so you have complete freedom to write whatever you want. There are no rules, except to fill those three pages each morning! It may seem a little long at first, but in return you can start to build a link with some of your innermost thoughts. Julia Cameron suggested that you don't reread your writing until eight weeks have passed.

So how about getting started on that? Get hold of a brand-new notebook, and start today (even if you don't have a notebook yet).

WHAT DO YOU THINK OF THIS?

....

....

....

....

....

....

....

....

....

....

....

....

....

The vision board

Sometimes also called a **dream board**, this is a collage of images that frequently forms part of personal development projects. Your images and words are gathered from magazines and stuck onto a large sheet of cardstock, based on a theme. The idea is for you to create a vision board that will allow you to put your objectives into visual form, finding images to represent your own hopes, desires, and aspirations. It can become a powerful tool in helping you make your inner dreams more tangible.

HOW ABOUT STARTING WITH THE HOUSE OF YOUR DREAMS? OR ANOTHER THEME, IF YOU'RE FEELING INSPIRED.

Start out by going through old magazines, cutting out words and pictures that correspond with your specific dreams, ambitions, or projects. Paste them onto a large piece of cardboard. If there are aspects missing, simply draw them in with a felt-tip pen. When you're done, take a photo.

ATTACH A PHOTO OF YOUR VISION BOARD HERE

The mind map

In their books on mind maps, authors Tony and Barry Buzan explain: *"A mind map, also called a heuristic map or a mental map, is a graphic representation of radiant thinking. Radiant thinking refers to the process by which the human brain generates ideas. The mind map reproduces and imitates this radiant thinking, which in turn can amplify natural brain function, making it more powerful…"*

How about creating your own mind map? First, write the word *creativity* and put a circle around it. Then draw ten branches. On each branch, write the first word that comes to mind when you thinking of the central theme of creativity. Don't cross out any words because you think they're "wrong."

If you find you have more words to add, just add more branches. The mind map can open the floodgates to the association of ideas, freeing up your imagination. If you're interested, read one of the Buzans' books, or research the idea online.

Creativity

ATTACH A PHOTO OF YOUR
COLLAGE HERE

Collage

Making collage is fun, relaxing, and anyone can do it. It takes away the pressure to get a specific result, and nobody is going to judge its merits. It's a great activity for anyone who is a bit anxious about their drawing ability. You get interesting results, and fast.

Gather up a bunch of images that inspire you, cut out of magazines, as well as words and phrases. Don't overthink this: just enjoy the fun aspect of it.

HOW DID IT GO?

....
....
....
....
....
....

Spontaneous drawing

Spontaneous drawing is where you allow a drawing to express how you're feeling at that specific moment. It can be extremely simple, like the drawings of a child, or just a line, a curve, a stick figure, a scribble, or splashes of color. There is absolutely no need to be "good at art."

Imagine yourself as a child, without a care in the world, just drawing freely. Start out by getting relaxed, then take a pen and draw directly in this book, whatever comes into your mind. And if your mind feels empty, start with just a dot, and simply add lines to it at random, perhaps adding color too.

WHAT WERE YOU FEELING?

....
....
....
....
....
....
....
....
....
....
....
....
....

Mandalas

The mandala is a drawing made within a circle, converging toward a central point. The name *mandala* is a Sanskrit* word meaning "circle, center, unit, totality." The circle symbol features across all cultures and traditions, both in East and West. It is a symbol of life: birth, adulthood, death, and resurrection or rebirth.

Drawing and coloring mandalas is a way of finding your own deepest inner center, with a sense of peace, calm, and concentration flowing out like energy. It is deeply meditative.

Have a go at drawing your own mandala. First, draw a circle in the book, marking the center point. Starting from there, draw the shapes or motifs that please you: flowers, plants, trees, stars, fish, or all kinds of geometric motifs… For inspiration, take a look at some of the amazing mandalas online. And finally, color in your mandala.

WHAT WOULD YOU LIKE TO CALL YOUR MANDALA?

....
....
....
....
....
....

*Sanskrit: the classical language of ancient India.

Creative visualization

Creative visualization is a mental technique that is related to self-hypnosis. It involves closing your eyes and trying to imagine—with great clarity and precision—what it is you wish to make happen during your life. In fact, the images that come to mind are so real that you can almost feel what it is like to be there. It is a technique that can be used in all aspects of life, and is particularly valuable in the creative field. To find out more, take a look at the pioneering work *Creative Visualization* by author Shakti Gawain.

HERE IS AN EXERCISE INSPIRED BY CREATIVE VISUALIZATION:

Find somewhere comfortable to sit (or lie down) where you won't be disturbed. Let your body relax completely, starting from your toes and working all the way up to the top of your head. Relax your muscles one by one, imagining all the tension draining from your body. Breathe deeply and close your eyes.

Imagine that creativity is a luminous presence standing before you. Feel this shining presence approach you and feel its warmth. Continue to breathe slowly and deeply, and imagine this presence is talking to you, warmly and lovingly. You hear their voice murmuring in your ear: "I need your help. I need you to help me express myself, to be my interpreter, because I know you can do it." Feel the joy this message brings you. Feel your heart skip a beat, and then speak the word out loud: "YES!" Imagine this presence is now smiling and gives you a special gift of thanks. Can you see what it is? Now they are leaving you with a final message, a wave, and they are gone. Stay in this scene for a few moments, before returning to yourself.

WOULD YOU LIKE TO WRITE DOWN WHAT YOU JUST EXPERIENCED? HOW DO YOU FEEL NOW?

....
....
....
....
....
....
....
....
....
....
....
....
....

Know how - to ask

The creative power of a simple question

Have you ever noticed how powerful a question can be? The simple fact of asking a question demands a response. And that creates a special kind of dynamic. If you ask a question, it implies a certain confidence that you'll get an answer. We have to be ready for when that answer comes: sometimes it is not exactly what we were expecting.

Asking a question is a more open way of thinking than simply trying to solve a problem. In fact, it takes away some of the pressure and opens the door to creativity. Have you ever noticed this in your life, and if so, how?

WHAT PROBLEMS ARE YOU GRAPPLING WITH IN YOUR LIFE RIGHT NOW? HOW ABOUT FRAMING THEM IN THE FORM OF A QUESTION?

....
....
....
....
....
....
....
....
....

Knowing how to ask for help

If you try to surround yourself with people who are going to support you in your project to reconnect with your inner creativity, then you will find you can draw more easily on your own inner resources. Try to avoid those who want to take control of your creative plans, or who try to solve all your problems with ready-made solutions. When you're in the middle of the creative process, and you need to seek advice, take some care over who you ask.

DO YOU KNOW HOW TO ASK FOR HELP? AND WHO WOULD YOU ASK?

....
....
....
....
....
....
....
....
....

If you find you have few people around you who can support you in your creativity, think about asking for help from the universe—ask life itself to help you meet the kind of people who can support you.

WHAT ARE YOUR THOUGHTS?

....
....
....
....
....
....
....
....
....

Listening for answers

If you ask a question, you also need to be able to listen for the answer. And often, inspirational answers can come right out of the blue.

Sometimes, you get so caught up in a question that you're convinced the answer will be found in a certain place, and you can miss it. Knowing how to listen for answers requires a belief that the answers are out there somewhere, plus the flexibility to accept answers that don't even look like answers!

Have you ever been seeking an answer to something and found what you wanted unexpectedly, perhaps in a book, or a phrase you heard on TV, or a chat with some friends, or even in a dream?

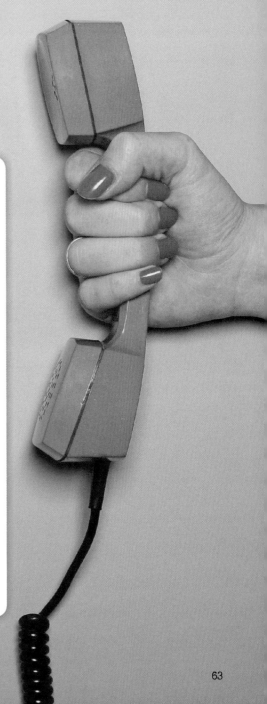

WRITE DOWN SOME EXAMPLES.
WHAT IS YOUR MOST FREQUENT WAY OF FINDING ANSWERS?

....
....
....
....
....
....
....
....
....
....
....
....
....
....
....
....
....
....
....
....

Reformulate the question

Here's an alternative. Instead of asking yourself why you're not managing to do something. Ask yourself instead what you need to do to get the result you want.

Think about a problem you're facing at the moment. Write the question down in your notebook. For example: "How could I put more creativity into this area of my life?" This evening, put your notebook next to your bed, along with a pen, and ask for help from within yourself, somewhere deep within you.

Try to write your request for help as precisely as possible. Have confidence in the universe at large: it will respond to you through some kind of sign or intuition, or perhaps through a chance encounter...

HOW DID THAT GO? WHAT DID YOU NOTICE?

BE ON THE LOOKOUT FOR ANSWERS, HOWEVER THEY MAY APPEAR. NOTE THEM DOWN OVER THE COMING HOURS AND DAYS, AND REPEAT THE EXERCISE IF YOU NEED TO. THINK OF IT LIKE A KIND OF FITNESS TRAINING, REINFORCING YOUR CAPACITY TO FIND ANSWERS TO QUESTIONS, OPENING YOUR MIND TO ANYTHING THAT COULD LINK BACK TO WHAT YOU'RE SEEKING.

Why?

This is almost like a magical question, which can change everything. Ask yourself what's really important to you, and then ask why it matters. This can apply to your creative life and to the rest of your life. Ask yourself what really counts for you, and why.

Make a list of 20 or 30 questions starting with "Why?" This may seem to be a lot, but it will help you start thinking about whether what you want is really important to you—or, in some cases, perhaps not.

Asking the universe

Close your eyes and get comfortable. Imagine that somewhere in the universe there is an immense reservoir, a huge lake, or an inland sea, and that the answer you're seeking exists somewhere in this expanse of water. You arrive at the edge of this vast sea, and you ask your question. You have an absolute certainty that the answer to your question is here, and you're going to draw out a response. All you need to do is stand there, and the answer will, eventually, come to you. Allow time for the answer to come: it could take hours, or even days.

Note down all your ideas, even those that do not seem to provide any kind of direct answer. Perhaps in those ideas you will find the elements of the answer you seek.

WHAT WAS THAT EXPERIENCE LIKE? CAN YOU WRITE ABOUT IT?

....
....
....
....
....
....
....
....
....
....
....
....
....
....
....
....
....
....
....
....
....
....
....
....
....

Creative workshop

This time, you can try a more creative way of asking your questions.
Imagine a character from a fairy tale, living in a different world, in another dimension,
but who is experiencing exactly the same kinds of problems as you.
Imagine they create their own magic formula.

WHAT QUESTIONS DO YOU THINK THEY COULD BE ASKING? WRITE YOUR STORY IN THE SPACE BELOW.

Welcoming new ideas

DAY 78

So many ideas

It can get stressful sometimes, having to come up with an idea. We end up creating too many filters: an idea has to be a really good idea, it needs to wow everyone who hears about it. Thinking like this actually makes all the good ideas disappear.

Finding an idea is more about developing a receptive attitude, where you can let a lot of different thoughts come in without instantly judging their worth. In fact, we live our lives surrounded by ideas. But do we even notice them? **Ideas are everywhere, much nearer at hand than we think.**

DO YOU THINK IDEAS ARE HARD TO COME BY? THAT IT'S HARD TO HAVE IDEAS? THAT THERE AREN'T ENOUGH OUT THERE FOR EVERYONE? OR THAT ONLY SOME PEOPLE CAN HAVE THEM? ARE YOU RECEPTIVE TO IDEAS? DO YOU DISMISS THEM TOO EASILY?

....
....
....
....
....
....
....
....
....
....
....
....
....
....
....

Finding the dynamic

Seeking and discovering ideas is a kind of mechanism. But it is also like a muscle that we can exercise. The more you go out looking for ideas, the more you will find. More concretely, here are some of the stages that seem to be important in finding ideas:

- **Stage 1:** Work out what it is you want to find, and in what context. Be precise about what this is about.

- **Stage 2:** Put yourself into a state where you are open to receiving ideas. Be open-minded, flexible, and relaxed.

- **Stage 3:** Observe carefully what's going on around you, and note what you see without judgment.

- **Stage 4:** Sort through what you've found and decide what to keep.

FOR A SPECIFIC PROJECT, DESCRIBE WHAT YOU'RE LOOKING FOR IN TERMS OF IDEAS. WHAT COULD HELP YOU BE MORE RECEPTIVE TO ANY IDEAS THAT COME IN? PERHAPS A WALK, OR SOME MUSIC, OR A MEDITATION?

....
....
....
....
....
....
....
....
....
....
....
....

Some useful techniques

HERE ARE SOME STRATEGIES TO HELP GENERATE IDEAS:

• BRAINSTORMING

Typically a group exercise, brainstorming focuses on a specific subject and ideas are allowed to come up in the free flow of the group and simply noted down, without filter or judgment, even if there is no obvious connection. The sorting out happens later.

• YOUR INNER CHILD

Another way of finding inspiration is to visualize your inner child, and ask them to participate with you in the project. Ask what they would do, in your place, and what they would like to create.

• ASKING THE UNIVERSE

You can also use the process described on Day 76: Asking the universe.

• WRITE IT DOWN

Get a good notebook and designate it as your ideas book, noting down moments of inspiration as they arise. Note 'em, or lose 'em!

WHICH TECHNIQUE WILL YOU USE TODAY TO START TO GATHER IDEAS? WRITE DOWN YOUR THOUGHTS.

....
....
....
....

Free your mind

If you feel a bit confused after an intense session of brainstorming, sometimes the best way to fix on an idea is to leave everything behind and go for a walk. Try to get your mind to calm down, and forget about whatever it was you were searching for. It is often at this precise moment of letting go that an idea can emerge—often when you're least expecting it!

WHAT CAN YOU DO TO MAKE YOURSELF REALLY RECEPTIVE TO IDEAS? WRITE DOWN WHAT FEELS BEST FOR YOU.

....
....
....
....
....
....

WHEN DO YOU USUALLY COME UP WITH IDEAS? IN THE SHOWER? ON A WALK? BEFORE FALLING ASLEEP?

....
....
....
....
....
....
....

DO YOU REMEMBER HOW YOU GOT YOUR BEST IDEAS EVER? WRITE DOWN HOW IT HAPPENED.

....
....
....
....
....
....
....
....
....
....

Ideas and originality

We often expect our creative ideas to be unique and original, but when you think about it, most ideas are not like this at all. What makes them appear original is the way they associate one idea with another, via your own unique interpretation. It's the part you play that makes the idea feel new and unusual. It's a bit like cooking: people can bake with the same ingredients and end up with completely different results.

The important thing is not so much the originality of the idea, but what you do with it. Think about how many painters have depicted landscapes, or portraits, or still lifes, but each in their own distinct way.

Originality comes from making links between ideas. As Steve Jobs said, *"Creativity is just connecting things. When you ask creative people how they did something, they feel a little guilty because they didn't really do it, they just saw something. It seemed obvious to them after a while. That's because they were able to connect experiences they've had and synthesize new things. And the reason they were able to do that was that they've had more experiences or they have thought more about their experiences than other people."*

WHAT CAN YOU TAKE FROM THIS IDEA IN YOUR OWN CREATIVE LIFE?

....
....
....
....
....
....
....
....
....
....
....
....
....
....
....

Ideas are searching for you

Suppose ideas exist somehow as actual things, with their own independent life. It may sound rather fanciful, but it can be a useful way of thinking about them, and one that author Elizabeth Gilbert explores in her book *Big Magic: Creative Living Beyond Fear*. For Gilbert, these ideas have just one mission: to find a human willing to show these ideas to the world.

Perhaps the idea that you're searching for is also searching for you!

WHAT DO YOU MAKE OF THIS IDEA? DOES IT INSPIRE YOU? NOTE DOWN YOUR THOUGHTS.

A creative dream-state where ideas can flow

Here is a meditation exercise that may help you capture those ideas. You're going to give yourself the space and time to really open yourself up to creative ideas on a subject that is close to your heart.

First, create a suitable space, calm and quiet, perhaps with candles or incense, or go out into the garden or a park in the summer. Keep a notepad alongside you. Let your thoughts drift, with nothing particular in mind, and watch your thoughts going by, like butterflies on a warm summer breeze.

If you have a thought that you like, that inspires you, make a note of it. Be kind to yourself, not critical. See where your ideas are taking you and welcome them with warmth and kindness.

WAS THAT EASY OR DIFFICULT? DID YOU ENJOY IT? WRITE ABOUT THE EXERIENCE BELOW.

....

....

....

....

....

....

....

....

....

....

....

....

....

....

....

....

....

....

....

The powers of observation

DAY 85

Seeing with fresh eyes

The ability to observe what's around you is an essential part of creativity. How you see the world helps define who you are, and developing your powers of observation can be enriching, making you feel more closely tied to everything around you. This in turn is linked with your capacity to be in the moment, with an openness and curiosity, ready for adventure and discovery. If you can see the world with fresh eyes, you can discover a new taste for life.
And with a new taste for life comes the desire to create!

TAKE A FRESH LOOK AT THE WORLD AROUND YOU.

Imagine you're just "passing through" the life that you lead, sticking around for just a few weeks in your neighborhood. What would you want to do if you knew you had to leave town in just four weeks' time? What things have you always wanted to do? What would you regret not doing if you had to leave town for good?

....
....
....
....
....
....
....
....

SUPPOSE YOU HAD TO ORGANISE A PARTY WITH YOUR FRIENDS—DO YOU HAVE SOMETHING CREATIVE IN MIND? WRITE ABOUT IT HERE.

....
....
....
....
....
....
....
....
....

A blue day

Today, for the whole day, you're going to aim to see nothing but the color blue.

Spend the whole day looking for anything and everything that is blue (or any color you want—no matter!). Let your gaze wander across everything that you encounter today, in search of this single color. Maybe go out for a walk. Immerse yourself in a blue world.

IN YOUR NOTEBOOK, WRITE DOWN EVERYTHING YOU SEE THAT IS BLUE. AND HOW WAS YOUR BLUE DAY TODAY?

....
....
....
....
....
....
....
....
....
....
....
....
....
....
....
....
....
....
....
....
....
....
....

An extraterrestrial point of view

If you really want to engage with the creative process, but are afraid that your life feels a little too ordinary or dull, then try looking at it in a completely different way.

Imagine you're an extraterrestrial tourist who has just showed up in your neighborhood. Imagine what they will make of your world, your home, your life. For the whole of this day, try to see your life as they might see it. Make some notes, remember the sounds and odors, tastes, colors, and feelings. If you feel inspired, make some sketches or collages.

HOW WAS THIS DAY FOR YOU?

....
....
....
....
....
....
....
....
....
....
....
....
....
....
....
....
....
....

In touch with your senses

Observing the world not just with your eyes, but with all your senses, allows you to experience the world in a completely new way. Today, you're going to try to connect with the world through the medium of paint. (And it could get messy!)

Take a very large sheet of paper and plenty of water-soluble paint. Forget about paintbrushes—you're going to use your hands, elbows, feet, nose, anything, to get paint onto paper.
Take time to enjoy this crazy moment, and feel like a child discovering paint for the first time.

WHAT WAS THE EXPERIENCE LIKE? HOW DID IT FEEL?

....
....
....
....
....
....
....
....
....
....
....
....
....
....
....

A change of perspective

Imagine today you're a bird flying over your life. Close your eyes and feel yourself flying, looking down over where you live. You can see yourself down there, going about your daily jobs. What does that feel like? Take some drawing materials and draw yourself, like a bird up there in the sky, and then draw where you live, seen from the sky.

HOW DOES THAT MAKE YOU FEEL?

....
....
....
....
....
....
....
....
....
....
....
....
....

How your inner child sees it

Close your eyes, get in touch with your inner child, and invite them to guide you through the day so you can experience your life as they might see it. Let yourself be inspired, to touch and to see the beauty, poetry, and magic in the world around you.

DESCRIBE YOUR EXPERIENCE. WHAT DID YOU NOTICE, AND WHAT DID IT FEEL LIKE? DID YOU LEARN SOMETHING ABOUT YOURSELF?

....
....
....
....
....
....
....
....
....
....
....

Taking stock

**Congratulations! You have reached the end of your first 13 weeks. Bravo!
You can be really proud of yourself.**

Look back at the journey you have made since the start of this book. It's not bad, right?
What do you make of it so far? What have you learned about yourself?
What's changed or evolved? Do you see aspects of progress?

TAKE TIME TO REVIEW HOW THINGS HAVE GONE SO FAR, AND TO CONGRATULATE YOURSELF FOR GETTING THIS FAR. HOW WILL YOU CELEBRATE?

....
....
....
....
....
....
....
....
....
....
....
....
....
....
....
....
....

The creative attitude

DAY 92

Keep on searching, keep on learning

Of course, we don't all wake up one morning and say: "That's it! I'm creative now! I can now stop all this because I'm done!" To be creative is really about cultivating a certain kind of creative attitude, which is something that never stands still—rather like the way nature never stands still, with everything constantly growing, regenerating, and evolving. Your creativity, then, is something that has to be "always on"—meaning you're always keen to discover, experiment, and learn, in all kinds of new areas. You can always take your creativity further, into new areas, across new horizons. So how do you learn? Where do you get your knowledge? **Write down your sources of knowledge, as well as the areas where you would like to learn more and deepen what you know.**

WHAT FIRST STEP IN THIS VENTURE COULD YOU MAKE TODAY? AND CAN YOU PLAN AHEAD, WITH A FIRM DATE IN YOUR DIARY?

....

....

....

....

....

....

....

....

....

....

....

....

....

....

Create
what you love

If you create with your heart and soul, then your creations will come alive and make you feel alive in the process. Austin Kleon, in his book *Steal Like an Artist,* expresses it perfectly in one beautiful sentence: "Draw the art you want to see, start the business you want to run, play the music you want to hear, write the books you want to read, build the products you want to use—do the work you want to see done."

WHAT CREATIONS WOULD YOU LIKE TO SEE IN THE WORLD? WHAT DO YOU HOLD CLOSE TO YOUR HEART? MAKE A LIST, EVEN IF IT SEEMS CRAZY OR IMPOSSIBLE!

....
....
....
....
....
....
....
....

Stop taking yourself so seriously!

Just be yourself! Allow yourself to mess things up, to be bad at things, to have fun, to laugh at your faults and weaknesses. Doing this will create fertile ground for creativity, freeing your mind and making you way less self-critical. **So relax: creativity is not a life-or-death struggle.** We all tend to put art and artists on a pedestal, and can easily forget that being creative is just a human trait that we all have. And nobody can take that away from you.

HOW COULD YOU PUT MORE LIGHTNESS AND HUMOR INTO YOUR CREATIVE LIFE?

Did you laugh today? What could you do to laugh a little bit more? Maybe tickle the kids, make faces in the mirror, or just have 15 minutes of craziness?

....
....
....
....
....
....
....
....
....
....
....
....
....
....
....
....
....
....
....
....

Staying passionate

We can sometimes think that to achieve our creative goals, we have to be passionate about creativity and nothing else. In fact, this is the wrong way to look at it. Being passionate about one thing can reinforce your passions for another. What's more, giving time to the other things you love will give you a welcome break from your creative focus, which in turn can be a time when you can pick up some of your best new creative ideas. This is especially true for things you do just for the pleasure of it: not to win or lose or be judged, but to enjoy.

WHAT THINGS ARE YOU PASSIONATE ABOUT—PERHAPS OUTSIDE OF YOUR CREATIVE FOCUS?

If you have many, which are the most important, and have the most meaning for you? How can you manage the time you have to be able to enjoy all the activities that you love??

....
....
....
....
....
....
....
....
....
....
....
....
....
....
....
....
....
....

Stop complaining!

Complaining is about the least creative thing we can do, as it brings us down
and stops us drawing on our own inner resources to make things better.
So try to focus on what you really want to have, rather than what you really don't want.
Forget the idea that your creativity needs to take place in some predetermined set of
ideal conditions. Just go with what you've got.

HOW OFTEN DO YOU COMPLAIN ABOUT THINGS?
SUPPOSE YOU COULD USE THAT ENERGY IN ANOTHER WAY?
WHAT WOULD YOU DO WITH THE SPARE TIME IT GIVES YOU?

The discomfort of change

Change is not necessarily easy to deal with, but it can also prompt us to change ourselves too. In our lives we often have to negotiate crises that force us to make changes, and that can show us the limits of our ability to adapt. Ultimately, if we accept change as best we can, knowing that things will eventually get better, then these kinds of changes will be easier to deal with.

Do you have trouble accepting change? Why is that? Can you remember some major changes in your life and what you learned from them? Have there been big changes in your creative life too? How did you deal with them? Did things ever turn out better than you expected?

WRITE ABOUT IT HERE.

Dance practice :-)

Make sure you're in a quiet place with plenty of space. Put on some music. Close your eyes, take a deep breath, and imagine creativity as a real person, right in front of you.

Now ask them for a dance. I mean, really … yes, you read it right!

Hold out your hand and invite them to dance. They accept. With your eyes closed, feel the energy right alongside you and start to dance with them. Let yourself go, and dance for as long as you want. When you want to stop, come back, gently, to yourself.

WRITE ABOUT HOW THE EXPERIENCE WAS FOR YOU. WHAT DID IT FEEL LIKE? YOU CAN DO THIS DANCE AGAIN, OF COURSE, WHENEVER YOU WISH.

. WEEK 15 .

Feeling playful

DAY 99

Rediscovering play

Creativity can be seen in its purest form in the simple pleasures of play. We're going to try to rediscover this sense of play, something that was so natural during our childhoods, and which can make us, as adults, both happy and more creative.

Close your eyes and take a deep breath. Visualize your inner child and invite them to sit alongside you and draw something with you. Use your *other* (nondominant) hand to create a childlike drawing of you in the space on the right. Focus simply on the pleasure and the fun.

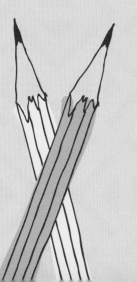

HOW DO YOU FEEL? WAS IT DIFFICULT?

....
....
....
....
....
....
....
....
....
....

Observation

Go into a park, find a bench near a playground, and watch the kids playing. Notice how they are totally immersed in the moment, right there in the middle of the games they are playing, absorbed in the pleasure of their own make-believe. Try to connect with that energy.

What kind of thoughts and feelings were evoked? Note them down, without judgment, welcoming whatever ideas come to mind.

....
....
....
....
....
....
....
....
....
....

NOW HAVE A GO AT PLAYING LIKE A YOUNG CHILD AGAIN—COLORING OR DRAWING IN THE SPACE BELOW. HOW DOES THAT MAKE YOU FEEL?

Your childhood games

Time to remember: do you remember the games you played as a child? Games played at home, in your room, maybe on vacation, or in the schoolyard. Maybe it was on the swings, coloring, dressing up, building something, playing with toy cars or a fire truck, riding your bike, roller skating, playing with your dolls—anything!

DO YOU REMEMBER HOW PLAYING WAS SUCH A PLEASURE?

Think about those games you used to play as a child, taking time to recall how much you used to love those kinds of games. Make a list of your favorite games.

....
....
....
....
....
....
....
....
....
....
....
....
....
....

Time to play

Reconnect with your inner child, and choose one of the games or activities in the list you wrote down yesterday—and get started! Try to feel that childlike pleasure in all its simplicity, and enjoy it to the fullest.

Let yourself become absorbed in what you're doing. Let yourself go!

NOW WRITE DOWN WHAT THAT WAS LIKE FOR YOU. WHAT DID YOU FEEL?

....
....
....
....
....
....
....
....
....
....

Letting play into your life

Do you leave any space for play in your life right now? Do you manage to let yourself play, just for the pleasure of it? Do you give yourself time to do this?

WHAT CHANGES WOULD YOU MAKE IN YOUR LIFE TO MAKE IT MORE PLAYFUL?

....
....
....
....
....
....
....
....
....
....
....

The creative playdate

How about inviting one of your close friends to stop by for a playdate? Who would you invite? Tell them about how you're involved in this yearlong creative journey, and think of something fun to do. Maybe a dress-up session where you take photos of each other. What do you think?

WRITE ABOUT THE EXPERIENCE HERE.

....

....

....

....

....

....

....

....

....

ATTACH A PHOTO OF
YOUR PLAY SESSION
HERE

How play can make
everything else easier

Suppose you could bring this playful aspect into your daily life, even into all the dullest and most repetitive tasks? Can you imagine, say, singing songs while stuck in traffic, drawing or coloring while you're in a waiting room, cooking up a meal with some kind of fantasy theme?

**HOW CAN YOU ADD A BIT MORE ZEST TO THESE EVERYDAY
TASKS—A BIT MORE PLAYFULNESS AND FUN INTO YOUR LIFE?
START HERE WITH A LIST OF IDEAS.**

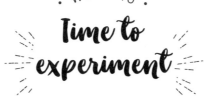

. WEEK 16 .
Time to experiment

DAY 106

Something new

New experiences are like fuel for creativity. This week, I'd like you to try out a whole load of new things for the first time. It's a chance to discover what you really like to do.

So what areas, subjects, techniques, or maybe sports would you like to get to know? It could be anything that you have never actually tried out. Suppose you had all the time and money in the world—what would you like to do then? How would you go about trying to do some of these things in your life right now?

Make a list, and do some research to see how to get started on some of these new activities. What's the first step? Make a date in your diary to do this..

THE DAY AFTER THAT DATE, WRITE DOWN WHAT HAPPENED.

....
....
....
....
....
....
....
....
....
....
....
....
....
....
....
....
....
....
....
....

Getting crafty

This time, set yourself the challenge of getting to know a new kind of craft activity. What would you want to try out? Sewing, knitting, crochet, embroidery, origami, DIY, woodcarving, calligraphy, photography? Or if you're really not into crafts, maybe you'd try out a new sport? Or start to learn a foreign language? The main thing is to try out something that is really new—rather than embarking on some activity that you don't like!

Is there a course or a workshop in your neighborhood? Check it out and sign up for a "taster course." Make the date in your diary. Alternatively, watch a tutorial online. How do you feel about starting out on this? Excited? Terrified? Not interested? And why is that?

WHAT HAVE YOU LEARNED ABOUT YOURSELF?

....
....
....
....
....
....
....
....

ONCE THE COURSE IS FINISHED, WRITE ABOUT YOUR EXPERIENCE: WHAT YOU LIKED OR DISLIKED. DO YOU WANT TO DO THIS AGAIN?

....
....
....
....
....
....
....
....

Excite your taste buds!

This time, I'd like you to head to a grocery store and buy something that you have never tasted before. Find out how to cook it and then see how it tastes. Alternatively, you could pick up a takeout meal from someplace where you have never eaten before, and try that out instead.

SUPPOSE YOU USED AN UNUSUAL INGREDIENT IN ONE OF YOUR RECIPES?

If you were baking a cake, could you spice it up with some chili? Or put a vegetable into a sweet dessert pie? Treat the kitchen as a laboratory, where you can test absolutely anything. What did you end up making? Take a picture and stick it into the book.

ATTACH A PHOTO OF YOUR CREATION HERE

WRITE ABOUT HOW IT WENT.

Other cultures

Obviously, we can't all jump on an airplane and fly halfway across the world just for the fun of sampling another way of living. So instead, how about getting a flavor of another culture by watching a foreign film? Or by going to an exhibition or gallery to see something that you would normally never have thought of seeing?

Do some research, stay open-minded, and pick out something to see or do. Make a date in your diary. Write down some more ideas for outings, and put the list in your creative happy box.

HOW WAS IT FOR YOU? WRITE ABOUT WHAT THOUGHTS AND FEELINGS CAME UP DURING THIS ACTIVITY. DID IT SPARK SOME CREATIVE IDEAS? SUPPOSE YOU WERE GOING TO ORGANIZE A REAL TRIP TO ANOTHER CULTURE? WHERE WOULD YOU GO?

Stuff you hate

This time, make a list of all the things that you don't like, asking yourself, for each one, why don't you like it? Have you tried it before? Are you sure you don't like it? Sometimes, as the years pass, we can completely forget why we don't like this or that, and our tastes can evolve over time too. You could take some of these things and try them again, just to see if you feel the same way. Make a list of the things you really dislike, which seem to be the opposite of who you are, or which you know nothing about and are totally uninterested in trying!

Now make a pledge to try a new experience. Choose something off your list, and plan a moment to try it out. Be open to the new experience, and maybe bring some friends—and your sense of humor!

DID YOU LOVE IT? OR HATE IT? WHY? WANT TO TRY SOMETHING ELSE?

Drawing with your eyes shut

Take a large sheet of paper and some markers. Close your eyes (or use a blindfold). Now have a go at drawing, whatever comes into your mind, even though you can't see a thing. It could be a tree, or flowers, or animals, or a fire truck, cars, people, a house... **But make sure you have fun!**

HOW DO YOU FEEL NOW?

Change colors, and carry on drawing for a little longer, still without looking. Now open your eyes and take a look at the result. Wow! Compare what you have drawn with what you thought you were drawing. Take a photo of your drawing and stick it into the book.

WHAT WAS THE EXPERIENCE LIKE FOR YOU?
WHAT ARE YOUR THOUGHTS?

....
....
....
....
....
....
....
....

ATTACH A PHOTO OF
YOUR DRAWING HERE

Review of the week

What did you make of this week full of "experimental" activities? Did you like it? Was it fun? Or weird?

Do you want to carry on experimenting like this? What other ideas do you have? Eat a meal in complete darkness? Go swim in icy water in a mountain lake? Do a parachute jump?

HAVE FUN BY ORGANIZING SOME MORE
NEW EXPERIENCES IN YOUR LIFE.
WHAT WILL YOU START WITH?

....
....
....
....
....
....
....
....
....
....
....
....
....
....
....
....
....
....
....
....
....
....
....
....

. WEEK 17 .
Feed your
Creativity

DAY 113

Nurture your project

The most beautiful illustration of the creative process, and how we can nourish our creative projects, is—to my mind—the image of a pregnant woman.

She carries her child for nine months, nonstop. Even if she is not thinking about the baby all the time, the seed has been sown, the process has begun, and everything within her body is working toward the development of this new person, giving them whatever they need in the best possible conditions. Meanwhile, she is also taking care of herself, because by doing this she will be taking care of the baby in the same way, and this provides a motivation to go above and beyond. She has a natural desire to give the best of herself. She will nourish the baby with food, but also with her thoughts and emotions. She will picture how the baby will be, lying in her arms, and all the great moments they might have together, all the love that she can give. And even while she may have to deal with fears, anxieties, and doubts, she will feed the baby with love, beautiful thoughts, and hope.

DO YOU HAVE A CREATIVE PROJECT?

How do you feel about the image of the pregnant woman in relation to your own project? How can you nourish your project, and with what? Will it be with things you read, or experience? Music you listen to, or films? What kinds of pleasures or pastimes will help your project evolve and grow, or what kind of training or expertise? What else can you think of?

DAY 114

Reading

Books can be a huge source of inspiration, whatever kind of things we like to read. So read whatever you love, and so much the better if it has nothing to do with your creative projects. It's just for the pleasure: nourishing you, and so nourishing your project.

WHAT COULD YOU READ ON YOUR FAVORITE SUBJECTS?

We're talking about books, articles, and blogs online. Who are the inspiring personalities in some of the other fields outside your specific creative area? See if you can find biographies on some of these people. Make a long list of books and websites that will provide inspiration for your reading over the months to come, whatever mood you're in. How can you get more information on the subjects you enjoy? How will you get started?

....
....
....
....
....
....
....
....
....
....
....
....
....
....
....
....
....
....
....
....
....
....
....

Inspirational creators

Today we're going to try an exercise from Austin Kleon's book *Steal Like an Artist*. First, choose someone you find inspiring and do some research on them, finding out everything you can—how they think, how they work. Then find three more people that this person in turn finds inspirational. Find out about them in the same way, and then, for each of them, find three more people that they find inspirational. You can use all kinds of sources, including online videos and interviews. You will be amazed how someone you find inspiring will lead you to others working in a completely different field. Keep exploring in this way, and see where it takes you. And if you get a chance to meet any of these people in real life, then go for it!

Now make a kind of "family tree": print out some pictures of the various creative people that inspire you, and then cut them out and arrange them in the form of a family tree (of who inspires whom). You can do this below, or on a larger sheet if you prefer. You could also add words or symbols to indicate what, in particular, each of these people is adding to your own creative mix.

Music

DO YOU LIKE MUSIC?

Music can be an incredible source of creative inspiration. Start by looking for music that will stimulate your creativity, either on the Internet or elsewhere, and maybe put together some playlists: to keep your spirits up, for fun, for relaxation, or to boost your creative powers. What other themes might inspire you? You could even make a playlist to go with your current creative project: what do you think?

....
....
....
....
....
....
....
....

Here's an exercise to try. Choose some music that goes with how you're feeling right now. Get comfortable, and keep a notebook handy. Let the music wash over you, while thinking about your project, and then let your visual imagination free and see what images come to mind.

WHAT DID YOU EXPERIENCE?

What effect did this music have—did it allow you to come up with images, emotions, feelings? Note down what came to mind.

....
....
....
....
....
....
....
....
....

Travel

Travel is a great way to feed your creativity, giving you time to relax, replenish, and to restock your creativity (by not being overtly creative!). Do you like traveling? Even a simple change of scene can be enough. Have you already made any trips that proved to be really inspirational and fed into your desire to create? Sometimes taking time off from creating can be extremely creative too!

ARE YOU PLANNING A TRIP THIS COMING YEAR? IF SO, WHERE?

If you're not planning to get away, then how about doing something else instead: try out a restaurant you have never tried before, perhaps with food that is way outside your usual comfort zone. What would you choose? And what micro-voyage might you be able to make this very day?

....
....
....
....
....
....
....
....
....
....
....

A visual feast

DAY 118

Do you get a sense of being nourished and enriched by seeing beautiful things? Maybe you want to surround yourself with images that inspire you? Who are the painters, photographers, designers, and makers who inspire you the most? Is it important for you to be surrounded by beauty in your inner life? Do you feel the need to get out and experience the beauty of nature?

MAKE A LIST OF YOUR FAVORITE KINDS OF IMAGES. HOW CAN YOU USE THESE KINDS OF IMAGES TO FEED INTO YOUR CREATIVITY? WHAT STEPS WOULD YOU NEED TO TAKE?

....
....
....
....
....
....
....
....
....

DAY 119

Time to play

To be creative, you need to take time off for recreation and play. Go out with friends, spend time with your family, share a meal someplace. Take another look at Week 15, which was all about play, and write down any new ideas that will help you recharge your batteries.

HOW DO YOU RECHARGE YOUR BATTERIES? HOW CAN YOU GET MORE PLAYFULNESS INTO YOUR LIFE? HOW WOULD YOU START?

....
....
....
....
....
....
....
....
....
....
....

WEEK 18

Free yourself

DAY 120

Freedom

Our freedom lies in the choices that we make. **Making a choice means giving up something, so that we keep only what is important and meaningful to us.** At the same time, not making a choice is a way of refusing the freedom that we do have. What does freedom mean to you, and in which aspects of your life would you like to enjoy more freedom? What would it be like if you were completely free in terms of your creativity? What would your life be like?

DESCRIBE WHAT TOTAL CREATIVE FREEDOM WOULD MEAN TO YOU.

....
....
....
....
....
....
....
....
....
....
....
....
....
....
....
....
....
....
....
....
....
....

Dare to push beyond your limits

DAY 121

SO WHAT'S STOPPING YOU? DO YOU FEEL THERE ARE LIMITS TO WHAT YOU CAN DO? IF SO, WHO SETS THEM? WRITE DOWN WHAT COMES TO MIND.

....
....
....
....
....
....

HOW COULD YOU BREAK THROUGH THESE BARRIERS?

How could you use creativity to push through some of the limitations listed above? Close your eyes and take a deep breath. Let your imagination float freely. **Note down anything that comes to mind, and if nothing emerges right now, don't worry about it. You've set the thought in motion.**

....
....
....
....
....
....
....
....

DO YOU FEEL LIKE WRITING ABOUT THE EXPERIENCE, OR PERHAPS PAINTING SOMETHING?

....
....
....
....
....
....

Freedom to be yourself

DAY 122

No need to make excuses for the choices you've made, the things you do, and the person you have become. Instead, dare to be who you are! Feel the freedom of saying what you think, and claim the right to lead a creative life! Think about how many times you have said things like, "I'm not very good at this, it's not perfect," all the time wishing that things were different.

Now is your chance to think differently, and to be fully, unconditionally, yourself. Take ownership of your own limitations—and then decide to ditch the lot of them!

HOW CAN YOU FEEL FREER TO BE YOURSELF? TRY GIVING YOURSELF MORE FREEDOM TO CREATE. SEE WHAT HAPPENS, AND NOTE IT HERE.

....
....
....
....
....
....
....
....
....
....
....
....
....
....
....
....
....
....
....
....
....
....
....
....
....

DAY 123

Your best-ever moments of freedom

CAN YOU REMEMBER TIMES IN YOUR LIFE WHEN YOU FELT REALLY FREE?

Here's an exercise. Close your eyes and try to remember times when you felt really free. Think about these memories: the time and place, and what happened. Write down your recollections in as much detail as you can, trying to really feel that freedom once again. Perhaps you can remember times when you felt you had excelled, going beyond your limits. These are precious moments in our lives, revealing the best of our abilities, and giving us incredible energy.

NOTE DOWN SOME OF THESE MOMENTS IN THIS BOOK, OR IN A NOTEBOOK, OR IN YOUR CREATIVE HAPPY BOX. YOU MAY WANT TO REREAD THEM WHEN YOU FEEL THE NEED.

A creative freedom workshop

Take your notebook or a sheet of paper and deliberately spill a bit of coffee on it. Yes, really! Have fun with the coffee stains, and see what you end up with. Enjoy making a mess, and then dry the paper and take a look at the marks that are left. What can you create, starting from these? Maybe some animals, or flowers, or faces, if you add some eyes, maybe a moustache. Stick the sheet of paper into the book. How was the experience for you?

DON'T LET THE EDGE OF THE PAPER HOLD YOU BACK! YOU CAN CONTINUE YOUR DRAWINGS, OFF THE EDGE OF THE BOOK AND STRAIGHT ONTO ANOTHER SHEET OF PAPER. HOW DID THIS GO? WAS IT EASY OR DIFFICULT? DID IT FEEL LIBERATING? WHAT EFFECT DID IT HAVE ON YOU?

....
....
....
....
....

Not caring what people think

Would you go outside and hop down the street? Or open the window and sing at the top of your voice? How about chasing imaginary butterflies in the park? The way we're brought up often puts the brakes on crazy, imaginative stuff. But what if you had the freedom you enjoyed as a kid?

In the list below, weigh up how you'd feel about doing any of the suggested activities, and tick the box that corresponds with your feelings.

	☹	🙁	😐	🙂	😌
A TICKLING SESSION					
SKINNY DIP IN THE LAKE					
SHOUT IN THE PARK					
DANCE LIKE YOU'RE CRAZY					
SING A STUPID SONG VERY LOUDLY					
GO OUTSIDE IN A COSTUME					
JUMP IN PUDDLES					
WALK INTO THE SEA FULLY CLOTHED					

Suppose you decide you're going to have a go at one of the things on the list. Get your inner child to join you. Which of these would they choose? How do you feel about doing that one? It's all about ignoring whatever other people might think of you, which could be easy … or not. If you think of other ideas, add them to the list.

HOW DID YOU FEEL ABOUT THIS EXERCISE?

....
....
....
....
....
....
....
....
....
....

Freedom day

TODAY IS THE IDEAL TIME TO OFFER YOURSELF A MOMENT OF PURE FREEDOM: IT'S YOUR BONUS DAY!
Read back in your notes about when you felt true freedom. Try to get in touch with this powerful feeling, and to enjoy the benefits of that today.

WHAT WILL YOU CHOOSE TO DO TODAY TO SHOW HOW FREE YOU CAN BE?

....
....
....
....
....
....
....
....
....

Tame your fears

DAY
127

What are you afraid of?

Fear is the signal that arrives in our brain when we sense danger is imminent. It is instinctive, and we can end up in a kind of paralysis, unable to go any further, unable even to think. In the moment, our fears can be completely disproportionate to whatever it was that triggered them, and we wind up being more afraid of the fear than of the thing itself! But taking a closer look at our fears allows us to get some distance from them. (If the questions below make you uneasy, take a break.)

MAKE A LIST OF WHAT YOU'RE AFRAID OF:

For example, fear of the unknown, fear of change, or of emptiness, fear of failure, or even fear of success? Fear of a lack of ideas and inspiration, or of not being up to the task? What if you were living your creativity as fully as possible: are you afraid of that too? If so, why? And what are you most afraid of, out of all of these? What is the worst that can happen in your creative life?

....
....
....
....
....
....
....
....
....
....

Fear has its uses

DAY
128

Bob Proctor, an author and motivational speaker, once said: "If you're not a bit afraid, then it could be that you simply don't want it enough." Hidden behind our greatest fears we can often find our greatest dreams, and maybe it's only right that they cause us anxiety because of how much they matter to us. To realize our dreams we are going to have to go above and beyond what we thought we could do, and in doing that we can reveal the very best of ourselves.

Fear, though, has a useful side in helping us plan our projects. It forces us to think about the risks involved, and exercise caution before plunging headfirst into the unknown, saving us from losing time, money, and more.

Do any of your own plans or projects strike fear in your heart—and I mean real fear? What in particular, and why? Suppose your fears had a useful role, warning you about something. Take a moment to think about how your fears may be serving a purpose and note down any thoughts that come to mind (and this may be tomorrow or next week).

HAVE YOU EVER FOUND THAT FEAR ACTUALLY HELPED YOU IN SOME WAY? WRITE ABOUT IT HERE.

....
....
....
....
....
....
....
....
....
....
....
....
....
....
....
....
....

The fear monster

The following exercise can help you distance yourself from your fears, and may even get rid of some of them for good. It is a simple exercise, but it can be powerful in its effects.

Choose one specific fear and think of it visually. Imagine your anxieties as terrifying monsters, with tentacles, slime, whatever. Now start to draw them, adding more detail as you go, possibly coloring or shading. As you go on adding arms, eyes, teeth, your terrifying monster will start to look more and more cartoonish, to the point where it's just plain ridiculous. Have fun, and let yourself go! When the monster is done, draw another. You may end up with the "fear of failure" monster and the "self-consciousness" monster and so on. Give them ridiculous names.

If you want to take this further, draw them on a separate sheet of paper and then destroy them—cut them up, scribble over them, or throw them into the fire!

HOW DO YOU FEEL NOW?

What was it like to do that? Was it fun? How do you feel now, thinking again about those fears? How do you feel about your monsters now?

....
....
....
....
....
....
....
....

Fear of change

Our fear of change often leads us to resist change. We are fearful of that leap into the unknown, and prefer to stay in the comfort of what we know, even though we can't see and don't fully understand what it is we're afraid of. But suppose the act of conquering our fears could lead to unexpected benefits?

Do you have a dream in mind, a big project that you would love to do, but that makes you fearful at the same time? What is it all about? What is the prize, if you were able to get there? Is there, alongside your fears, an equally powerful sense of excitement? One that is drawing you in, tempting you? Could you let go of your fears, and go way out of your comfort zone?

TRY TO IMAGINE THREE DIFFERENT SCENARIOS ABOUT WHAT COULD HAPPEN IF YOU CONQUERED YOUR FEARS.

....
....
....
....
....
....
....
....
....
....
....
....
....
....
....
....
....
....
....
....

The antidote to fear

When it comes to your creative projects, the antidote to fear is to simply get on with the job. It's a bit like stage fright: intense when the actor is backstage, but often disappears when they go on in front of the audience. If fear (of failure, of mockery, whatever) becomes a real blockage for you, try to approach the problem from another angle. Think how river water can simply flow around a rock and then continue on its path to the sea!

Is fear holding you back? Time for some diversionary tactics! Instead of fretting over your project, do something else that you find fun and inspiring: bake a cake, go for a walk, read a good book. It will do you good to let go of things for a short while, to kick back. Being in the moment and doing something that gives you pleasure will help build back your resources and give you more energy when it comes to picking up where you left off.

Another way to fight through the fear is by not giving yourself any choice in the matter. Don't overthink things, and take the first small step toward the work that needs to be done. Pick up on the first idea that comes to you (it doesn't have to be original or exceptional) and work with that. Don't make the best, as they say, the enemy of the good.

WHAT'S THE WORST THAT CAN HAPPEN? WHAT WILL YOU DO TO GET STARTED AGAIN?

....
....
....
....
....
....
....
....
....
....

The fear of mistakes

The fear of mistakes is really a fear of being exposed as not good enough, and is a serious block to our creativity. But mistakes themselves are precious things. We can learn from them. And they act like way markers: go this way, not that way. So it's worth getting on good terms with our mistakes. Don't see them as failures, with the sense of powerlessness that brings. Instead, think of the various errors, false starts, and U-turns as containing vital information, all of which will help you become more expert and experienced in what you do.

Allow yourself to make mistakes and to enjoy experimenting. There is no "wrong way" when it comes to play. There is just your own way!

ARE YOU AFRAID OF MAKING MISTAKES? WHAT ARE YOU AFRAID OF?
HAVE YOU EVER MADE A MISTAKE THAT TURNED OUT TO BE USEFUL?
WRITE ABOUT IT HERE.

....
....
....
....
....
....
....
....
....
....

CAN YOU THINK OF A MISTAKE RECENTLY THAT YOU FELT WAS A SETBACK?
HOW CAN YOU LOOK AT IT DIFFERENTLY, AND WHAT DOES THIS TEACH YOU?

....
....
....
....
....
....
....
....
....
....

Who do you want to be?

DO YOU KNOW THIS POEM BY MARIANNE WILLIAMSON?

Our deepest fear is not that we are inadequate.

Our deepest fear is that we are powerful beyond measure.

It is our light, not our darkness

That most frightens us.

We ask ourselves,

Who am I to be brilliant, gorgeous, talented, fabulous?

Actually, who are you not to be?

You are a child of God.

Your playing small

Does not serve the world.

There's nothing enlightened about shrinking

So that other people won't feel insecure around you.

We are all meant to shine,

As children do.

We were born to make manifest

The glory of God that is within us.

It's not just in some of us; it's in everyone.

And as we let our own light shine,

We unconsciously give other people permission to do the same.

As we're liberated from our own fear,

Our presence automatically liberates others.

Do you find this poem inspiring? Our inner fears challenge us to search deeper within ourselves, and show us that rather than stopping us in our tracks, they are helping us to grow and evolve. They help us tap into a rock-solid inner confidence, so that we can give the best of ourselves in all we do.

IN THE SPACE BELOW, DESCRIBE AN EXPERIENCE YOU HAVE HAD IN YOUR CREATIVE LIFE, WHERE OVERCOMING A FEAR LED YOU TO DISCOVER A SENSE OF GREATER INNER CONFIDENCE AND POWER.

....

....

....

....

....

....

**IF YOU CHOSE TO LIBERATE YOUR INNER STRENGTHS, WHAT WOULD BECOME POSSIBLE?
DO YOU WANT TO BE PARALYZED BY YOUR FEARS, OR DO YOU WANT TO FACE UP TO THEM AND GO THROUGH THEM,
BECOMING STRONGER AS A RESULT? DURING YOUR LIFE, WHAT FEARS WOULD YOU LIKE TO OVERCOME?**

....

....

....

....

....

....

Have courage

Workouts for courage

DAY 134

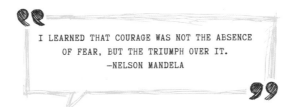

> I LEARNED THAT COURAGE WAS NOT THE ABSENCE
> OF FEAR, BUT THE TRIUMPH OVER IT.
> —NELSON MANDELA

Courage won't stop you feeling fear. But it will help you get through it. And you can think of it like a muscle, which you can work out with exercise, by setting yourself challenges to overcome and leaving you feeling good about yourself.

How about setting yourself a "Courage Day" once a month, when you will give yourself a challenge, doing something you did not feel you were capable of? Start by making a list: for example, talking to a stranger, singing as you walk through the mall, or making an important phone call that you've been putting off for weeks. It doesn't have to be big stuff, but it needs to be important for you. Pick one out and put it in your diary for this week, and then, when the day comes, do it. Write down what it was like.

HOW DO YOU FEEL NOW?

....
....
....
....
....
....
....
....
....

Creative courage

Being creative takes courage—the courage to be yourself, to show what you're all about. We put a lot of ourselves into our creations, and it takes courage to show the world what we have made. There is always the risk of criticism, but if we avoid this, we end up never making any progress.

Being creative means having the courage to persevere, to get back up and start over, learning all the time from setbacks and never giving up on the original creative dream. It means being willing to ask yourself hard questions, to own your mistakes, and to be ready to change your perspective.

HAVE YOU BEEN ABLE TO SHOW CREATIVE COURAGE? WRITE ABOUT WHAT HAPPENED, HOW IT FELT, AND WHAT YOU LEARNED FROM IT.

....
....
....
....
....
....
....
....
....
....
....
....
....
....
....
....
....

Courage versus perfection

If you want to be sure of doing a perfect job before you start anything, what do you think will happen? The short answer is: nothing. Try to find the courage within yourself to get started even if you don't feel up to it, and you will see how simply getting started will energize you. You'll discover that as you move forward, the creative life you seek will come to meet you.

CAN YOU RECALL MAKING A LEAP INTO THE UNKNOWN THAT TURNED OUT TO BE WAY BETTER THAN EXPECTED?

....
....
....
....
....
....
....
....
....

Creativity without limits

Make a list of creative projects or activities that excite you, but which are also a little scary: perhaps they feel a bit ambitious, as if you may want to do them later rather than sooner. You dream one day of doing them, and you admire people who can.

Now choose something from your list, and start it today. Yes, really! If it seems too big to do all at once, divide it into a series of steps and make a start.

WHAT FIRST STEP COULD YOU TAKE TO ENCOURAGE YOURSELF TO GO BEYOND YOUR LIMITS? WHERE WILL YOU START?

....
....
....
....
....
....
....
....
....
....
....
....
....
....
....
....
....
....
....
....
....

Playing the joker

What would best symbolize the notion of courage for you? Choose someone, or something, that you feel has the right kinds of qualities, and let's get creative.

Take some paper around the size of a postcard and draw your chosen character, using colors and collage as you wish. Have some fun adding all the courageous qualities that you feel are important. This will be like your joker card in the deck of your creative life. Pull it out whenever you need some extra help dealing with those creative fears that stand in your way. On the back of the card, write a motivational quote.

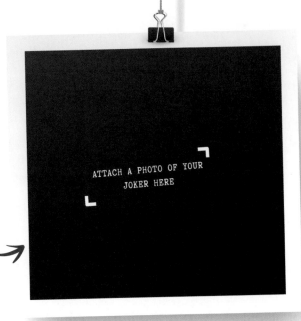

ATTACH A PHOTO OF YOUR
JOKER HERE

Courageous moments

Try to remember some of your successes in life, when you have had to use all your resources to overcome a challenge, achieving something you never thought possible. When you have something in mind, reflect on it, trying to recapture what it felt like.

Write about it in your notebook. Where did it happen, and what was going on? Describe what it felt like at the time, and see if you can recapture that feeling now as you think about it again.

HOW DID YOU FEEL WHEN YOU MANAGED TO OVERCOME THAT CHALLENGE?
Try to use these memories to inspire you on days when you need to find all your courage.

....
....
....
....
....
....
....
....
....
....
....
....
....
....

An encouraging letter

Today, you're going to write a letter to help and encourage your inner child. Imagine you're helping them overcome some kind of challenge. What would you like to say to them to get them to push themselves to new limits and reach success?

CONGRATULATIONS!

YOU HAVE REACHED THE END
OF WEEK 20. YOU CAN BE
PROUD OF YOURSELF!

Overcoming creative blocks

DAY 141

Creative blocks

The creative life rarely flows smoothly. There are often unexpected bumps in the road that can easily throw us off track. As Julia Cameron puts it in *The Artist's Way*, "A successful creative career is always built on successful creative failures." Even the most celebrated creatives have experienced their own blockages, dead ends, and false starts. But is it a creative block, or is it just a phase in the creative cycle—a kind of seasonal hibernation when nothing seems to happen on the surface, but when ideas area quietly fermenting?

The best bet is to accept these creative blocks for what they are: temporary stops, a bit like stations or bus stops, or way markers on the route. You can go past them, or sort them out, or change them: it's you in the driver's seat, after all. You can choose to see them as obstacles, of which you are the victim. Or you can see them as an invitation to think about what you're doing, ask yourself questions, and take your ideas even further forward.

DO YOU FEEL LIKE YOU HAVE A CREATIVE BLOCK?

Have you just abandoned a project after running into an obstacle? Was this after a big mistake, perhaps a kind of "self-sabotage"? Have you abandoned projects midway through? If so, what happened? Looking back, can you see how you could have moved on, and maybe grown from the experience? Write your thoughts here.

Creative trauma

Everyone at some stage has a kind of creative trauma, something that happens that stops you in your creative tracks and that you can never put behind you. Can you remember a day when someone criticized you in front of other people, perhaps when you had done a drawing or made something you thought was good? Have you been harshly judged, or humiliated, or felt shame over something you tried to create?

Take some time to reflect on this, but above all, be kind to yourself. This exercise may spark some difficult memories and unpleasant feelings. Take your time, and try to examine the feelings that come up.

WRITE DOWN WHAT EMERGES.
And if nothing comes up, go back to Week 10 to help ask your unconscious to release some of these buried memories. Note down anything that comes to you over the next week, without judgment.

....
....
....
....
....
....
....
....
....
....
....
....
....
....
....
....
....
....
....
....
....
....

Back to the past, and a healing process

Freeing up a creative block can unleash energy that has been trapped in a past episode of your creative life and give you renewed vigor, enthusiasm, and desire to live your present-day creative life to the fullest. Whatever negative stuff people may have told you in the past about your creativity, here is a chance to lay those hurts to rest, and to reconnect with your deep, inner creative drive that will be the source for everything you do today.

Here is an exercise: try to remember some kind of creative setback during your childhood or teen years. Close your eyes and take your mind back to when the event took place. Look at yourself at the time, and think about what happened. Replay the scene. Let your ego—in this past moment—express your anger, frustration, and perhaps incomprehension at the situation.

Now try to explain to this younger self—with your adult perspective—that this was not their fault. For example, if they had been harshly criticized, you could explain that it was nothing to do with them, or what they had done, but that someone around them had felt somehow threatened by this spirit of creativity and had lashed out. If that person had realized just how hurtful their reaction had been to your younger self, they would have acted differently. Try to picture the scene as it might turn out differently, if you—the adult—were there to defend your younger self. Say the words you would like to have heard said at that moment, and embrace your younger self with love and compassion.

HOW ARE YOU FEELING AFTER THAT? IT TOOK SOME COURAGE TO GO BACK THERE, DIDN'T IT?

....
....
....
....
....
....
....
....
....

A hidden gift

CAN YOU REMEMBER A PARTICULAR CREATIVE BLOCK?

Did you manage to overcome it or not? A creative block encourages us to look at the situation from another angle. If there is some kind of benefit hidden beneath each creative block, what was it in this case?

Thinking back, what was the biggest obstacle to your creativity during your childhood and adolescence? Why? And what effects has that had on you since?

Write down what you remember about all this. Do you have regrets? How can you spot the hidden gift within each blockage, and change how you see the situation?

....
....
....
....
....
....
....
....
....
....
....
....
....
....
....
....
....
....

Creative block? Be creative!

Perhaps the best means of overcoming a creative block is creativity itself. After all, setbacks and false starts are not necessarily signs that a project is doomed. It could simply be that the timing is not quite right, or the method is not ideal, or some other detail is slightly off. The way through this is to stop thinking and start doing, returning to what drives you creatively. So grab a notebook, a pen, or your camera, and go outside for a change of scene. Come back with a sense of why you want to create, and write down any ideas that emerge. Suddenly, you're back on track!

TRY TO IMAGINE HOW A CREATIVE BLOCK
COULD LEAD TO A CREATIVE SOLUTION.

In the following exercise, try to imagine a magic flower, a symbol of what creativity might mean for you. It is a rare and mysterious bloom that has the power to remove all obstacles from your creative path. Imagine how it might look, its colors and form. Does it resemble a flower you have seen? Maybe it is more exotic, with feathers or scales, or even stars. Now get absorbed in the simple pleasure of making a picture of it. How do you feel now?

....
....
....
....
....
....
....
....
....
....
....
....
....
....
....
....
....
....
....
....
....
....
....

Asking for help

Getting help from someone when you hit a creative block can save an amazing amount of time and get your creative energy back on track much more quickly than you would imagine. Just the act of talking through the problem with someone else can get you thinking about it differently, returning to your work with new energy. Think carefully about whom you talk to. If your creative block is linked with painful experiences earlier in your life, it may be best to get in touch with a counselor.

SO WHO WILL YOU ASK FOR HELP?
Once you have chosen someone, get in touch with them.

How did the meeting go? What did you feel you were able to take away from it?

....
....
....
....
....
....
....
....
....
....
....
....
....

Review

CONGRATULATIONS!
You have just completed an important week in this creative journey, and it may have been a bit of a rocky road emotionally.

What did you become aware of during the week? Have you noticed any particular changes, even if they are only small ones? What are you most proud of? Have you managed to shift a creative block? What kind of progress have you seen?

....
....
....
....
....
....
....
....

PAMPER YOURSELF: IT'S A WAY OF SHOWING YOURSELF YOUR OWN UNCONDITIONAL SUPPORT, NO MATTER WHAT. HOW WILL YOU MARK THIS DAY?

....
....
....
....
....
....
....
....
....
....
....
....
....
....
....
....

the *Ditch*
routine

DAY
148

Are you sleepwalking into your project?

One of the biggest traps on the creative journey is routine. It dulls all sensations, kills off morale, repels any kind of inspiration, and saps energy. We end up nodding off to sleep and then wondering where the day went. Of course, some of us can put up with routine better than others, and structure and regularity can be reassuring. But in creative terms, getting out of a routine can often be a welcome—or even crucial—change.

So how about getting out of your normal routine to be more present with yourself and those around you, and to get a new appreciation of the world?

HOW DO YOU REACT TO ROUTINE? DOES IT CURB YOUR CREATIVITY? AND HOW CAN YOU GET OUT OF A ROUTINE? ARE YOU STUCK IN A ROUTINE RIGHT NOW?

....
....
....
....
....
....
....
....
....
....
....
....
....
....
....
....
....
....

A creative routine

When we are creative, we can all too easily end up in a creative routine. We take on certain creative habits and reflexes, and don't want to let them go. The price we pay for this is we get less pleasure from our creative activities and feel less alive to creative possibilities—without at first realizing what is going on. Our brains goes to sleep, and the creative lights go out, as we keep doing the same old things in the same old way.

The sense of boredom that comes with this can be seen as a yellow warning light, urging us to change our path—to put more creativity into our lives.

WHAT COULD YOU DO TO MAKE SURE THAT YOU BEGIN TO SEE BOREDOM AS A WARNING SIGN, URGING A CHANGE OF DIRECTION? AND HOW CAN YOU PUT MORE CREATIVITY INTO YOUR LIFE? MAKE SOME NOTES HERE.

....
....
....
....
....
....
....
....
....
....
....
....
....
....
....
....
....
....

Break the habit

It is not always obvious how to get out of a dull routine, especially when you have been in it for a long time. But here, a little creativity can go a long way: making a small change in what you do can often be enough, so that you widen your horizons with renewed energy.

Think about the routines that exist in your own life, and make a list of them. Then think about how you can disrupt them a little. Suppose, for example, you lived a day back-to-front, starting with dinner! (If you have kids, they will love this!) Or take a completely different route to get to work. Or change how you dress. Think of all the ways you could live your life (just slightly) differently.

WRITE DOWN YOUR IDEAS, INCLUDING THE SMALLEST OF SMALL CHANGES. WHERE WILL YOU START?

....
....
....
....
....
....
....
....
....
....
....

The anti-routine

DAY 151

When you're feeling fresh and rested, sit down and make an "Anti-Routine" list. When you're done, put it into your creative happy box.

Get in touch with your inner child, and ask them for more ideas about putting some more magic into your life.

{ **HERE ARE SOME IDEAS TO GET YOU STARTED:**
GO TO A SHOW, JOIN A CHOIR, TAKE A PHOTOGRAPHY COURSE, HAVE A PARTY, MAKE A MOVIE BUCKET LIST, BROWSE THE LOCAL BOOKSTORE, VISIT A NEW NEIGHBORHOOD, PLAN A HOLIDAY, FIND A NEW CHALLENGE... }

MAKE A DATE TO DO ONE OF THE THINGS ON YOUR LIST AS SOON AS POSSIBLE.

....
....
....
....
....
....
....
....
....
....
....
....

Rekindle your enthusiasm

Routine can easily cause us to lose sight of what really matters to us. So the best way out of it is to reconnect with the things that you love doing. Put together a new list of "why" answers about your creative project, as you did on Day 63. Even if it's not in your power to change your daily life, you can change how you see it and how you live it.

Take a look at all the wonderful things in your life. Give thanks for your health, for having a roof over your head, running water. Let a sense of simple gratitude get your spirits up, and see how that can bring enjoyment back into your life. Now go and find an inspiring text to read. And put on some music!

**HOW DO YOU FEEL NOW? READY TO DITCH THE ROUTINE?
HOW CAN YOU REKINDLE YOUR ENTHUSIASM?
WRITE DOWN YOUR THOUGHTS.**

....
....
....
....
....
....
....
....
....
....
....
....
....
....
....
....
....

Routines and relations

Even our everyday relations with each other are not immune to routine. So why not put a bit of craziness into your relations with your family, friends, or your partner?

What could you do to change things around? How could you inject an element of surprise? What could you do differently?

LET YOUR IMAGINATION RUN FREE, AND NOTE DOWN WHAT COMES TO MIND. WHAT FIRST STEP WOULD YOU NEED TO MAKE? DECIDE TO GET THIS STARTED.

....
....
....
....
....
....
....
....
....
....
....
....
....
....
....
....

Explore your senses, reconnect with the now

This time, I'd like to invite you to focus your day on just one of your five senses, and see how this can take you out of the everyday. Which sense would you choose? Go through your day paying as much attention as possible to the sense you have chosen. How can you use this sense differently?

NOTE DOWN YOUR IDEAS AT THE END OF THE DAY, AND WRITE BELOW WHAT THE DAY WAS LIKE FOR YOU. WHAT DID YOU NOTICE? WHAT DID YOU LEARN?

....
....
....
....
....
....
....
....
....

Lose the doubts

DAY 155

You and your doubts

Can anyone be creative and NOT have doubts? No way! But don't we enjoy it when we feel we have complete confidence in ourselves and our abilities? Of course, too much doubt means we lose a lot of time in worry and indecision. But in small doses, doubt can be very useful in helping us ask useful questions of our work. When doubt becomes ingrained and systematic, and you have doubts about your right to be creative, then things can go downhill fast. Doubts create hesitations and vacillations, which stop us from working and can be exhausting, sapping energy that could otherwise be so creative. So stop! Try not to let these doubts hold you back.

What's your story with doubt? If you can try to define it, you may be able to remedy it too. Is it doubt in your abilities? Or your self-worth? Your competence? Your creative decisions? Your creative power? And why do you have these doubts? Do you doubt your projects, in their thinking, or execution, or chances of success? And do you allow others to doubt you too?

WHAT COULD YOU DO TO REDUCE ALL THESE DOUBTS?

Change your attitude

Doubts can often emerge from a kind of fatigue, when you're not 100 percent in the moment of what you're doing. Then it is time to go do something else, break up the routine, get some fresh air, and recharge your batteries. Doubts can be another kind of warning sign (like boredom) that it's time to take a break and check that you're still on the right road.

So you don't need to let your doubts and negative thoughts limit what you're doing and stand in the way of your creativity. Learn simply to switch your attention to something else. Focus on what you're good at, where your energies lie, on your plans and aspirations, and on the things that inspire you in your life. Shore up, if you will, your self-esteem, and you will find it to be the very best antidote to doubt.

Do you really want to become someone who is paralyzed by their doubts? Didn't think so. Think back to some of the doubts you have had before, and how you have chased them away with your own courage and actions. Have you seen the difference in energy you can experience when you overcome self-doubt, compared with when you feel it is overcoming you? Write below one of the biggest victories you have accomplished over your own doubts.

....
....
....
....
....
....
....
....
....
....
....
....
....
....
....
....

Doubting your doubts

Do you have doubts about your creative project? But suppose you try to look at things another way. Imagine that behind every doubt, there is a hidden message.

Think of a doubt that you may have related to your current project, and imagine it is sitting right in front of you. Close your eyes and take a deep breath, and imagine you ask this doubt what it has come to do for you. What is the reason for it being there?

Perhaps you simply need some time out to take a break and gather your strengths, maybe to clear your head. Or to feed, in some way, your creativity. Or to check that your project still has the special meaning you intended at the start. Maybe you need to pick up some new skills to reinforce what you're doing?

IMAGINE THE RESPONSES YOU MIGHT GET. TAKE SOME TIME TO NOTE DOWN WHATEVER COMES TO YOU. WHAT ARE YOUR THOUGHTS?

....
....
....
....
....
....
....
....
....
....
....
....
....
....
....
....
....
....
....
....

DAY
158

An antidote to doubt

Do you sometimes feel invaded by doubts? If the answer is yes, then it's time to take action.
How about inventing a special "self-esteem" antidote to short-circuit these pesky doubts, allowing you to get right on with your creative work? What do you think this antidote would be like? Maybe like a huge syringe, full of colorful serum? Draw a picture of it now, and cut it out. When those doubts start to crowd in, reach for the syringe and take a transfusion of self-confidence! Alternatively, you could find an object that reminds you of a time when you managed to chase away your doubts and stay firmly on your creative path.

WHAT KIND OF SYMBOLS MIGHT HELP YOU? NOTE DOWN YOUR IDEAS AND ENJOY DRAWING THEM. PLACE YOUR ANTI-DOUBT SERUM INTO YOUR CREATIVE HAPPY BOX, OR EVEN IN YOUR WALLET, CLOSE AT HAND, READY FOR ACTION!

....
....
....
....
....
....
....
....

Facing Mr. Doubt

There you go: another of those annoying little doubts poking their noses into your business. So here's a fun exercise to send them on their way. First, imagine what a certain "Mr. Doubt" would look like if he existed. Draw a picture of him on a sheet of thick paper, and then cut him out. Imagine you're a kid playing: what would you want to say to Mr. Doubt? Something along the lines of: "Get going, mister, back where you came from!" and show him the door. Or alternatively: "You know what? Let's talk about this later on, when I've had a break and can think more clearly. In the meantime, you can get going!"

By waiting until later to reflect on doubts or any kind of negative thoughts, it is possible that you'll feel better able to deal with the issues at hand. **You could also try this:** visualize Mr. Doubt sitting opposite you and talk directly to him (though obviously not if you're surrounded by people in your office, or in the middle of a meeting!). You may feel a bit ridiculous doing this, but it can be pretty effective, and laughing at ourselves never did anyone any harm.

DOES THIS WORK FOR YOU? HOW DO YOU FEEL NOW?

....
....
....
....

Critical voices

Mr. Doubt has a bunch of friends, who we can call The Critical Voices. I'm fairly certain you will have heard of these, voices that can drag you down, thoughts that end up making you doubt yourself. Reflect on these repetitive, knee-jerk thoughts that make you start to think you're not good enough, not ready, not up to the task … It is an important first step in being able to transform these negative thoughts. You won't succeed in doing this overnight, as it is a process and it takes time. But in identifying these critical voices within you, you will slowly be able to overcome them.

WHAT CRITICAL INNER VOICES CAN YOU IDENTIFY?

FOR EXAMPLE: "THEY CAN ALL DO IT, BUT I CAN'T!" DOES THAT SOUND FAMILIAR?

....
....
....
....
....
....
....
....
....
....
....
....
....
....
....
....
....
....
....

A letter to your inner child

Take a sheet of colored paper and write a letter to your inner child. Dedicate this moment to them, and give them encouragement: all the good advice that you yourself would have welcomed at that age to help boost your confidence and get on in life.

HOW COULD YOU HELP THEM DEAL WITH THEIR OWN DOUBTS?

Criticism, Judgments, and antidotes

DAY 162

The fear of criticism

It's hard to hear any kind of criticism. It can reach some of our deepest insecurities. Becoming overly sensitive to criticism means that we fear it so much that we pretty much give up, simply to avoid any kind of external judgment. Especially in creative work. When we lack confidence in ourselves, we are at our most exposed. We react as though our most cherished ideas and values are being trashed. Our need for support and approval from others gets mixed in with our fear of failure and perfectionism—making us feel personally targeted by any form of criticism.

But here's the good news: it's nothing personal. You're not the target. It's just your ego that is a little out of sorts: the part of you that wants to please everyone. But you can learn to deal with all this in a different way, essentially by "stepping out" of the things that you create—or in other words, to "dis-identify" with your creations, so that you can benefit from all those constructive comments, without being hypersensitive.

At the same time, you're probably your own biggest critic. Take time to gently observe how you react to your own work, whether you can be a harsh critic, telling yourself that your work is not good enough, not enough of this or too much like that. This observation is not about adding yet more criticism of yourself: it's about trying to find a calm, sustainable way to keep moving forward.

DO YOU TEND TO LISTEN TO THE VOICE OF A HARSH INNER CRITIC? DO YOU FEEL THE NEED TO PLEASE EVERYBODY? WHAT KINDS OF CONVERSATIONS DO YOU HAVE WITH YOURSELF?

Observation day

Today, keep a watchful eye on your inner critical self. Watch out for how you react when you don't manage to achieve what you want, and make a note of it. Act like an impartial observer, with no sense of judgment.

How many times did you criticize yourself today? What did you give yourself a hard time about? Was this fair? You were only doing your best! How was what you did not enough? When we tend to criticize ourselves, we often do the same to people around us (but don't judge yourself harshly for this very common tendency!). Do you have a tendency to criticize others? Do you think you would do better than them, in their place?

....
....
....
....
....
....
....
....
....

AT THE END OF THE DAY, READ BACK OVER YOUR NOTES. LET YOUR EMOTIONS COME TO THE SURFACE, AND REFLECT ON WHAT YOU'RE LEFT FEELING. WHAT HAVE YOU OBSERVED?

....
....
....
....
....
....
....
....
....
....

Transform that inner critic

With the help of the exercises you have done over the last two days, take some time to reflect on this inner critical voice. What kind of negative messages is this voice giving you? Make a list below.

....
....
....
....
....
....
....
....

Learn to start developing another voice within you, one that is warm, friendly, and supportive and that can transform these negative ideas. What would this other voice (think of it as your best friend) say to you? Look again at the critical comments you listed above, and see if you can transform each one into its opposite. Give reasons why these new ideas are valid.

For example: "I am useless" becomes "I am good at this" and give an example of an area where you're really competent.

Write in the new set of comments about yourself, and come back to this exercise as often as you like. It is work on your interior self that takes time and demands compassion on your part.

....
....
....
....
....
....
....
....

Get rid of the judge!

Today you can have a go at drawing a picture of this character inside you that is constantly judging what you do and finding you wanting, or useless, or a failure. How would you portray them: as a person, or as some kind of monster? Take a large sheet of paper and draw them as you see them, as big as will fit on the sheet. Let yourself go a bit crazy with this drawing. Now take a different color pen and draw them again, but smaller. And then draw them again and again, smaller each time, until they become nothing more than a dot on the page.

Now, take a colored pen and draw a dot that is going to symbolize the confidence you have in yourself. Now, reverse the process, drawing the symbol for your inner confidence bigger and bigger, until it fills the sheet. Stick the resulting images in this book or in your notebook. You could also choose to rip up your picture of the inner judge into tiny pieces, or throw it into the fire. So long, judge!

WHAT WAS THIS EXERCISE LIKE FOR YOU? HOW DO YOU FEEL NOW?

....
....
....
....
....
....
....
....
....
....
....
....
....
....
....

Critics everywhere

People can be pretty mean-spirited when it comes to criticizing others, and you will need to guard against letting this behavior get to you. Others may, with the best intention in the world, offer a well-meaning criticism that actually hits you right where it hurts.

So first up, don't allow yourself to be defined by criticism of your work. And second, remember that people who dole out harsh criticism of your work are often harsh critics with themselves too. Facing up to someone's creativity can leave some onlookers feeling all too aware of how little they have in this department. Sometimes the critic will lash out at you when what they really want to do is criticize themselves. They don't see you for who you are, but for the mirror that you hold up to them. Complex, huh?

Here's an exercise to try: draw a circle, and in the center draw yourself (a stick figure will do) and write in your name. Inside the circle, write the names of your most trustworthy friends, with the distance from the sketch of yourself indicating how close you are in real life. Outside the circle, write the names of people who are very much a part of your life, but who are not so much on your wavelength, and who could have the power to hurt you with their critical comments. Some may be family: people you love. The message here is to know who you're dealing with, and that sometimes you will need to protect yourself, even among those you love.

WHO WILL YOU KEEP IN YOUR INNER CIRCLE, AND WHO WILL REMAIN OUTSIDE OF IT?

....
....
....
....
....
....
....
....

CAN YOU RECALL BEING DEEPLY HURT BY HARSH CRITICISM? HAVING WORKED ON THIS TOPIC THIS WEEK, CAN YOU TRANSFORM HOW YOU SEE THE SITUATION?

....
....
....
....
....
....
....
....
....
....

An antidote to the critics

Compassion and kindness toward yourself can be a great defense against that harsh inner critic that we all have inside of us. Remember, you're doing the best you can with the means available and the mind set that you happen to have at the time. Don't demand the impossible from yourself, and leave perfectionism to one side. Faced with judgments and critics, you will need to reinforce your self-esteem, so I'd like you to reread Week 6, and perhaps do some of those exercises once more.

Try to focus on your values, the essence of who you are, and the things you love. Claim back your absolute right to make mistakes. Get back to a more flexible, "anything goes" self, and rekindle your sense of humor and playfulness. What step could you take to make this happen?

MAKE A NEW LIST OF THE THINGS YOU LOVE AND WHY YOU LOVE THEM. REREAD IT AS OFTEN AS YOU LIKE.

....
....
....
....
....
....
....
....
....
....
....
....
....
....
....
....

The power of positive criticism

Remaining open to positive and constructive criticism is a precious thing for any creative person. It leads us to grow and progress, and anything that does that is worth keeping. Someone else's view on our work is a chance to share our creative experience, and may put into words something you have been feeling but were unable to pinpoint. If you feel that friendly and constructive criticism is justified, then accept it gratefully, and it will help you move forward. We can't always see immediately if criticism is going to be of value or not: there is no gold standard. And sometimes a rather harsh criticism can be the key to a really valuable step forward in your work. So once you have put a Band-Aid on your bruised ego, think about the meaning and implications of those comments. Sometimes the harshest lessons in life can also be the most useful ones.

....
....
....
....
....

To be better at receiving criticism, we need to ask ourselves: how can this criticism be useful to me? And also: do I want to be right, or do I want to learn?

Another way of transforming how you see a criticism or judgment is simply to say thank you! It will allow you to put these difficult emotions to one side and help identify the good that can lie at the heart of such criticism.

CAN YOU THINK OF ANY CRITICISMS YOU RECEIVED THAT, IN THE END, TURNED OUT TO BE BENEFICIAL?

....
....
....
....
....

Change what you believe

DAY 169

Reboot your beliefs

Our beliefs tend to form from our repeated thoughts, based on the things that we believe to be true, drawn from our daily lives. We grow up in a family, an environment, a society, immersed in people's beliefs. Unconsciously, we have accepted that many of these are true for us too. This is why it is so difficult to be aware of our beliefs, to the point where we never even think to question them.

The act of revisiting—rebooting, in fact—our negative beliefs is a big undertaking that is impossible to do in one go. But it is worth doing, and there is much to gain. When we start to question all of our beliefs, we begin to spot those that may be holding us back. So it's time to press "reset": ditch those beliefs that are dragging you down creatively, and retain those that feel really aligned with who you are.

What do we mean by a negative belief? It is a thought that has no useful role, that can throw us into a vicious circle: I am useless, I will never succeed, I am a bad person. Or even something like: it takes luck to succeed in life, and I don't have any.

ARE YOU AWARE OF YOUR NEGATIVE BELIEFS?

What are they? Starting with the examples mentioned just now, write down as many kinds of negative beliefs that you can think of. Take time to let them rise to the surface of your awareness. Come back to the list in the days that follow, if more ideas emerge.

Beliefs and creativity

Watch for how a simple belief can hold you back: if you believe that you're no good at painting, how can you ever see yourself standing in front of a canvas holding a paintbrush and paint, embarking on something completely new? The negative belief kicks in on an unconscious level, and is an effective (and invisible) block to you trying something new. But ask yourself: who told you that you can't paint?

What are your beliefs relating to creativity? Have they changed at all since you started this book? Take time to look through the responses you have written in this book and in your notebook. Are some of these beliefs evident? Note them down if you spot them.

Use the questions below to help you to make a list. Do you think that being creative casts a shadow over others? Can it put you at risk? Will being creative lead you to quit your job? Take a moment to look at your beliefs both in your everyday life and in your creativity. Do you have some fixed beliefs about creativity and money, or success, or careers? Or creativity and family? Or with your friendship groups? Or your health? Or creativity and spirituality? Or creativity and your love life?

START YOUR LIST, AND FINISH IT OVER THE COMING WEEK.

Put your beliefs to the test

Questioning your beliefs—all of them—will allow you to get back into the driver's seat, and decide for yourself how you want to live. We often think that something is true because the facts seem to support it, without realizing that we operate a kind of filter that allows in only those facts that support what we want to believe. So to change a belief, we will need to be open-minded enough to accept that there may be facts out there that contradict it. And that the opposite belief is valid, too.

Take responsibility over where you're headed. Choose what you believe. Otherwise, other people will choose for you and you will lose all power in your life. So challenge your beliefs by asking, first of all: how is this belief about creativity useful to you? What effect does it have on your life? Do you really have to believe that? When you see how useless some of your beliefs may be, it is much easier to drop them.

FOR EACH OF THE BELIEFS ON YOUR LIST, ASK YOURSELF HOW USEFUL THEY ARE FOR YOU. WHICH ONES WILL YOU KEEP?

Interrogating your beliefs

Here is a whole series of questions to help you to get to the bottom of your beliefs. Choose those that inspire you the most, or use all of them: the aim is to help you challenge your beliefs. Take your time, and try to be thorough.

WHAT BENEFIT DO YOU GET FROM THIS PARTICULAR BELIEF?

Do you really want to think of yourself as useless? Suppose you set out to find detailed proof that you were useless, with concrete examples. What event would have led you to this belief? Where does the idea come from? Who was involved, and how? What does it mean, to be "useless"? Where do you think you have failed? Have you already succeeded at stuff too? In what? What does that signify, in practical terms? Why do you think you're useless? Do you have what you need to succeed? Enough time to act, or to learn? Are you in good shape, mentally and physically? Are you prepared?

> { PUTTING A SETBACK INTO CONTEXT, LOOKING AT ALL THE FACTORS INVOLVED, CAN HELP NEUTRALIZE NEGATIVE BELIEFS. }

WHAT EVIDENCE CAN YOU FIND IN YOUR LIFE THAT DISPROVES SOME OF YOUR BELIEFS? WHICH BELIEFS CAN YOU LOOK AT IN THIS WAY?

WHAT LESSONS CAN YOU DRAW FROM THIS?

... AND IF YOU WANT TO KEEP BELIEVING SOMETHING, THAT'S OK. IT'S YOU WHO DECIDES!

Worst-case scenario

Imagine that one of your negative beliefs has survived all your attempts to disown it. What now? Suppose you try to imagine what would be the worst-case scenario if you were to no longer hold this belief. For each answer you think of, try to think of something even worse, and then even worse than that. This, I can guarantee, can become a hilarious game that will take all the sting and drama out of the situation. Have fun with this!

SO WAS IT REALLY SO BAD, TO DITCH THAT BELIEF? TRY IT WITH SOME OTHERS. WHAT CAN YOU CONCLUDE FROM THIS?

The writing cure

When it comes to changing your beliefs, the written word can be a surprisingly powerful tool. Your brain will record what you write, and it can be great way to reprogram ingrained beliefs. What's more, you could shift the focus to positive beliefs, which will provide stimulus and energy.

Looking at each of the negative beliefs that hold you back, write down their opposites. Now see if you can find evidence in your life to support these opposite views.

FOR EXAMPLE: "I'M NOT CAPABLE OF DOING …" WILL TURN INTO "I AM CAPABLE OF … THANKS TO …"

HOW DO YOU FEEL NOW?

Act "as if ..."

For this exercise, you can adapt the example below to suit your own creative project. It will work for any project, based on an initial scenario in which you have a negative belief that is blocking what you want to achieve. Imagine that you have chosen (for example) to paint a portrait, but you feel totally lacking in skill. You really want to do this, but it scares the hell out of you! Now we're going to do a creative visualization exercise in which you're going to behave "as if" it was within your powers. This will strengthen your self-esteem and ability to go beyond your limits.

So get comfortable, close your eyes, and take a deep breath. Imagine the room around you, perhaps as an imaginary space. Observe what's around you.

Now imagine the subject you wish to paint: your model. Take time to look at them carefully, imagining how the light strikes their face and sensing the feelings that are evoked in you. Now you're choosing a canvas, feeling its grain with your hand, and now you're taking a paintbrush, sensing its weight, balance, the feel of the brush hairs. Take up the palette, and start to squeeze out the paint, mixing the colors, smelling its odor. How are you feeling now?

Observe yourself sketching out the initial lines of the portrait, and from here, visualize in the same way all the stages of creating the painting, as if you were really there, right through to the finest details. Be alive to your emotions, mindful that on this emotional level, your brain will make no distinction between what you imagine and what you're actually experiencing. And the further you go with this, the better you will feel about yourself.

WHEN YOU'RE FINISHED, COME SLOWLY BACK INTO YOURSELF. HOW DO YOU FEEL? WHAT WAS THE EXPERIENCE LIKE? DO YOU NOW FEEL LIKE DOING IT FOR REAL?

....
....
....
....
....
....
....
....
....
....
....
....
....

Affirmations

DAY 176

The power of affirmations

Positive affirmations can be powerful tools for helping transform our negative beliefs, and can actually change the way we think. Our thoughts create our own sense of reality, and by modifying our thoughts we have a chance to change our sense of this reality. But to work with this tool, we need to be aware of how we are thinking most of the time, which is not so simple. We have to take responsibility for our thoughts so that we can then reprogram them: turning negative thoughts into positive ones, and repeating a phrase—the affirmation—to get it to sink into our subconscious, until it becomes a new thought and a new reality for us.

WHAT DO YOU THINK OF POSITIVE AFFIRMATIONS? HAVE YOU USED THEM BEFORE? HOW, AND WHY, AND WHAT WERE THE EFFECTS? WRITE ABOUT ONE HERE.

....
....
....
....

Today, try to observe what you're thinking about. Use a small notebook to note down what you're thinking at stages of the day, and what the theme is: work, family, money, etc. Is it a positive or negative thought? If it helps, use an alarm every hour and ask the same question. At the end of the day, complete your list.

DID YOU HAVE ANY SURPRISES?

....
....
....
....
....
....

{ I BELIEVE IN AFFIRMATIONS }

POSITIVES

Write down your affirmations

Take a look at your list of thoughts, and see if they are positive or not. Can you see any new negative beliefs creeping in? Do you want to try to deal with them? Which parts of your life are you dealing with here? Your relationships, work, health? Think about your beliefs, and those negative thoughts, and turn them into positive affirmations. Take a look at the examples below:

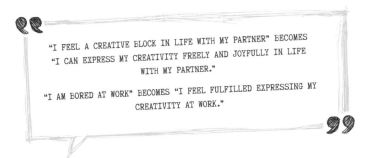

"I FEEL A CREATIVE BLOCK IN LIFE WITH MY PARTNER" BECOMES "I CAN EXPRESS MY CREATIVITY FREELY AND JOYFULLY IN LIFE WITH MY PARTNER."

"I AM BORED AT WORK" BECOMES "I FEEL FULFILLED EXPRESSING MY CREATIVITY AT WORK."

WRITE DOWN YOUR BELIEFS, AND THEN YOUR AFFIRMATIONS.

....
....
....
....
....
....
....
....
....
....
....

Try to sense the difference in energy you get from these positive and negative affirmations. You're on track to create new habits of thinking, simply by repeating these positive affirmations over a period of 21 days. If you repeat these affirmations mechanically without belief, you'll waste your time.
Say it with feeling, and you will feel the difference.

Affirmations for creativity

Take some inspiration from the list below to draw up your own set of creative affirmations. Choose those that resonate with you, and add more if you like. Make a list of your top 10 favorites, print them out, and keep them close by—or in your creative happy box.

I love to learn new skills.

Creativity flows freely within me.

I allow creativity to make itself felt throughout my life.

Every day I do something creative and fun.

The people around me support my creative life.

I feel good when I can express creativity.

I have all the time I need to express my creativity.

Now choose just one of these phrases, and adapt it however you want: the main thing is that it truly resonates for you. When you feel the need, repeat it, like a mantra, so that it seems to become deeply absorbed in your mind and, just as importantly, within your heart. Continue the exercise until you feel your energy levels starting to rise.

WHICH AFFIRMATION DID YOU CHOOSE?

....
....
....
....
....
....
....
....
....
....

IDEALLY, REPEAT THE EXERCISE DAILY FOR 3 WEEEKS. GIVE IT YOUR BEST SHOT!

Illustrate your affirmations

Choose three or four of your favorite affirmations and illustrate them. Start by writing them out on some drawing paper, perhaps in color, or using calligraphy, or print them out with fancy fonts. Maybe draw a frame around each of them, or add some collage or drawings. Have fun with this, so you can associate a good experience with the affirmations you have selected.

When you're done, place your affirmations in different parts of the house, or slip them into your diary or a book you're reading, or leave them in your car: anywhere you can find them easily, read them, and repeat them. Where will you put yours? Take a picture of them, and stick it into your book.

WHICH AFFIRMATIONS DID YOU CHOOSE?
WHAT WAS THIS EXERCISE LIKE FOR YOU?

....
....
....
....
....
....
....

ATTACH A PHOTO OF YOUR AFFIRMATIONS

Say it out loud

Take your list of positive affirmations and make an audio recording or a video of yourself reading them out loud (use your phone or computer). You could add some inspiring music in the background. Listen to your recording regularly, perhaps several times each day, for 21 days. Note down anything you observe while listening to these affirmations. Remember, you can add to your list of affirmations anytime.

HOW DO YOU FEEL NOW?

....

....

....

....

....

....

....

....

....

....

....

....

Pick a card

MAKE YOUR OWN FLASHCARDS

Spend some time to pick out your top 15 to 20 affirmations. Now cut up some drawing paper or cardstock into identical rectangles roughly 6 x 4 inches. Write your affirmations in color on one side of the cards (a different one on each) and add some decoration. Then paint the back of all your cards the same color. When you're done, take a photo of your set of cards and stick it into the book.

Each morning, pull out a card from the stack and repeat its affirmation throughout the day. Write in your notebook any thoughts that come to mind as a result.

ATTACH A PHOTO OF YOUR
CARDS HERE

Congratulations! Halfway there!

AWESOME!

You're now halfway through the year! And you can be proud of yourself!
In any case, I am really proud of you! What a journey! What do you think?

Have you stopped to think about what kind of progress you have made since
starting out on this journey? What have you noticed? Take some time to go
back through the first half of this book—and your notebook—and see how
things have evolved.

HOW WILL YOU CELEBRATE THIS TODAY?

Just for fun

DAY
184

A day of discovery

How about going out and buying some spices you've never tried before? Smell their aroma, and try to imagine where they're from and the journey they made to get to your kitchen. What feelings do they evoke? What would you make with them?

Now, suppose you add them to egg yolk to make paint! Have fun experimenting with cocoa powder, beetroot juice, paprika, curry... Try out your homemade paints on some art paper.

IN A WORD: HAVE FUN!

WHAT WILL YOU PAINT WITH THESE CONCOCTIONS? WHAT WAS THE EXPERIENCE LIKE FOR YOU?

....
....
....
....
....
....
....
....
....
....
....
....
....
....
....

Bonus day

DAY
183

Congratulations! To celebrate getting to this point in the year, let's have a whole week of recreation, with a bunch of activities aimed solely at your own fun and discovery.

And to start with, have a bonus day! You can use this to do whatever you like! Go out, take a walk, get some fresh air. Maybe it's something very easy to organize: something unexceptional but which makes you smile and puts a spring in your step. At the end of the day, write down what it was like.

....
....
....
....
....
....
....
....
....
....
....
....
....
....
....

Listen to your feelings

For this exercise, you will need some paint and a large sheet of thick paper. Choose some colors and mix the paints however you like. Take a deep breath, and then enjoy the simple action of painting across the surface of the paper, without any particular image or idea in mind. Go slowly, as if you are in a slow motion video, and feel every sensation that comes to you as you do it.

Maybe you would prefer to paint squares, or triangles, or blobs of color. What colors did you choose? What was the result? Did you find it relaxing? Or stimulating? Did you enjoy it?

DESCRIBE WHAT YOU FELT.

....

....

....

....

....

....

....

....

....

....

....

....

....

....

....

....

....

....

....

....

....

Make a calligram

A calligram is a poem in which the phrases you write move across the page to form a drawing. Take a poem, quotation, or piece of text that resonates with you. Then lightly sketch out the shape that you will use—it could be something connected with the text itself, or totally unconnected.

Write the poem on the page, following the pencil lines, and watch as the written words form the shape. You can then erase the pencil marks when you're done.

HOW WAS THIS FOR YOU? DID YOU ENJOY IT?

....
....
....
....
....
....

Telling a story

Pick out an object from your creative happy box at random. And now tell its story!
You could recount where this object came from and where it's been—or perhaps make it the
hero of some kind of fairy tale. Maybe you want to draw or paint the object? In the space below,
write the story that you have come up with. You can think of this exercise as
a kind of creative warm-up!

....
....
....
....
....
....
....
....
....
....
....
....

Make it tactile

DAY
188

Time to get messy. Prepare some paint
and a large sheet of thick paper. Have
fun by touching the wet paint with
your fingers to feel the texture, or even
by getting it all over your hands, and
then—the best part of all—print or
smear the paint onto the paper in front
of you. Let yourself go with the feeling
this gives you, in a rare moment of really
becoming aware of your sense of touch.
What does it feel like?

WHAT WAS THIS EXPERIENCE LIKE FOR YOU?

....
....
....
....
....
....
....
....
....
....
....

Rainbow visualization

Immerse yourself in color. Close your eyes and imagine a huge red sun saturating you with color. Feel yourself soaking in the light. Breathe gently and feel the color being drawn into your body, your cells warming as they bask in the soft red light. Then do the exercise again, passing through all the colors of the spectrum.

WHAT DID IT FEEL LIKE? WRITE ABOUT THE MOMENT.

....
....
....
....
....
....
....
....
....

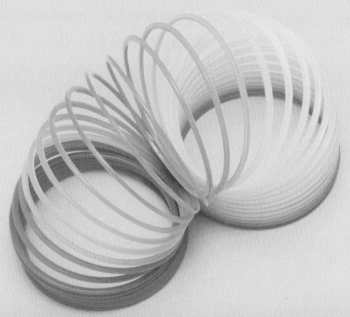

Transformation through creativity

DAY 190

Transformation through drawing

Using creativity to change how we feel about a difficult situation is a great way to connect with some powerful inner resources. This exercise is about short-circuiting your usual way of thinking, so go with your gut feelings and concentrate on the pleasure of creating something in the moment.

First, think about a tricky situation that you have to deal with right now. Summarize it in just a few words, and write them in the center of a big sheet of thick paper. Take your time, be kind with yourself, and then draw in some colorful flowers, hearts, trees, birds, stars, suns—anything that comes to mind that feels positive and uplifting— and use these elements to obscure the text. If you like, you can use paint or collage, transforming something difficult into a beautiful, colorful picture.

**HOW DO YOU FEEL NOW, COMPARED WITH AT THE START?
AND WHAT WAS DOING THIS EXERCISE LIKE FOR YOU?
TAKE A PHOTO OF YOUR PICTURE, AND STICK IT INTO YOUR NOTEBOOK.**

....
....
....
....
....
....
....
....
....
....
....
....

Transforming a relationship

Is there a relationship in your life that you wish was better? For this exercise, you'll need a sheet of paper and some colored pencils in all seven rainbow colors.

First, take a red pen and write the name of the person several times, so that your writing forms the first arc of a rainbow. Write it again above the first arc with your second rainbow color (orange), and continue like this until the rainbow is complete. Think about all the good aspects of this person, which will help transform your view of the relationship itself.

WHAT WAS IT LIKE TO DO THAT? HAVE YOU MANAGED TO SEE A SHIFT IN YOUR FEELINGS?

....
....
....
....
....
....
....
....
....
....
....
....
....
....
....

A mandala

Think about a difficult situation that you're dealing with. Take your colored pencils, and at the center of a sheet of drawing paper, draw a heart. Then move out from here to create all kinds of intricate and beautiful shapes you can color in later. Fill the page with your designs, and enjoy! Then start coloring, getting absorbed in the process until it is finished. Try to stay in the moment

HOW DOES IT FEEL NOW WHEN YOU THINK OF THAT DIFFICULT SITUATION AGAIN?

....
....
....
....
....
....
....
....
....
....
....
....

Change your perspective

What things do you NOT want to do? Make a list. For example: I don't to pay my bills, or the household chores, or go out this evening, or spend Sunday with my family. But suppose you could end up actually liking the things you don't like doing: what would that be like? How about using your creativity to change your view of all these things? What magical ingredient would make this transformation possible? It's not about forcing yourself to do something you hate. Rather, it's about changing your perspective on some of these things, seeing them in a new, positive way. You may decide that it is useful and enjoyable to bounce out of bed in the morning, but conversely, if you don't want to go out in the evening, you don't have to. So you can become clearer about how you decide what's best for you.

WHAT PRACTICAL WAYS CAN YOU THINK OF TO GO IN THIS KIND OF DIRECTION? NOTE DOWN ANY AND ALL IDEAS THAT COME TO MIND.

....
....
....
....
....
....
....
....
....
....
....
....
....
....
....
....
....
....
....
....

Repairing a situation

For this exercise, start by thinking about a rather painful moment in your life that has still not been completely healed.

Now lie down and close your eyes. Cast your mind back to the time of this memory and visualize who you were during this time. Begin a conversation with your inner self—the part of you that was hurt by the event in the past—and explain that you are ready to support them and help them get past this situation. Nobody is being blamed, and the events of the situation were painful because they were out of step with the expectations of your younger self. If others are involved, it is their own individual backstory that led to their incapacity to act appropriately or with more understanding or kindness.

Tell yourself now all the things that you would have liked to be told back then. When you're done, write those words down on paper. Then read them out loud.

HOW DO YOU FEEL NOW? CAN YOU WRITE ABOUT YOUR EXPERIENCE?

....
....
....
....
....
....
....
....
....
....
....
....
....
....
....
....

A ritual of transformation

Draw a big garbage can in the center of your sheet of paper, using the template below. Color it, and then cut it out. On a separate sheet, draw some rectangles. On each one, write a belief that holds you back, a negative thought, or a difficult situation you could do without. Cut out the rectangles and stick them on the drawing of the garbage can.

When you're done, fold the paper over to close the garbage can, and glue it in place. Then, choose a safe place where you can light a fire (the fireplace, for example). Focus your mind on your transformation, and then set fire to the paper garbage can and its contents.

NOTE DOWN WHAT YOU OBSERVED. HAS IT HELPED YOU TO MOVE FORWARD? IF SO, HOW?

....

....

....

....

....

....

....

....

....

....

....

LID OF THE GARBAGE CAN

FOLD & GLUE

FOLD & GLUE

Asking for help from the universe

Is there something blocking your creativity at the moment? In your notebook, write down the problem. And now ask for help from the universe, or from some higher power—whatever you prefer. How would you word your request? Have confidence, because the universe hears you, and will respond. Watch out for what happens over the hours and days that follow. Have you spotted any coincidences? Or any particular message? Has something caught your attention, in a phone call, maybe, or in a book? Can you relate that back to the question you asked in the first place?

NOTE DOWN WHAT YOU OBSERVED. HAS IT HELPED YOU TO MOVE FORWARD? IF SO, HOW?

....
....
....
....
....
....
....
....
....
....
....
....
....
....
....
....
....
....
....
....
....
....
....

Letting go

All about control

DAY 197

Creativity and control feel like they should be complete opposites. Control sucks the life out of creativity. Planning a route that is too controlled will trap your ideas, whereas letting go will allow a receptivity to new thoughts and concepts. Being flexible in your creative thinking is energizing. It allows that we can't have the whole picture, and there are many unknowns; by abandoning our fixed plans and ideas, we can enjoy creativity to the full.

Where are you in this process? Do you have a tendency to put yourself under pressure, controlling the process too much? Do you feel anxious about not knowing how things will turn out? Do you want to hang on to control, and in what areas do you notice this the most?

NOTE DOWN WHAT COMES TO MIND, WITHOUT JUDGING YOURSELF.

....
....
....
....
....
....
....
....
....
....
....

Training the "letting go" reflex

DAY 198

Managing events can feel reassuring, but in reality we are often working just to reduce our anxiety. So we can end up overcontrolling our creative projects in a bid to reduce anxiety, but this level of control is a great inhibitor of creativity, so we can end up feeling anxious about our lack of creative ideas!

Letting go is a practice that demands a certain amount of training, and in this exercise we will do a simple meditation that might help counter the anxiety that we all can feel about our projects. It's a quiet time, just for yourself. First, find somewhere comfortable to lie down. Is there a particular subject that is preoccupying you at the moment? Take a break, open up your mind, and just concentrate on your breathing. Now close your eyes and take a deep breath. Feel the tension in your body. Where is it located? Pass your entire body through your own imaginary mental scanner, taking your time as you work from your toes to your head. Breathe slowly and feel the tension dissipate as you focus on each area. If you were to add a color to the image of your body right now, what would it be?

HOW DO YOU FEEL NOW?

....
....
....
....
....
....
....
....
....
....
....
....
....
....

Your other hand

Here is an exercise to help you let go of the controls and stop yourself from overthinking, by making use of your nondominant hand. Take a deep breath and—please!—don't judge yourself. The aim of this exercise is to forget about "performance" while staying mindful of what you are feeling. First of all, choose some words that you find inspiring, such as "childhood" or "joy" or "enthusiasm," and write them several times using your nondominant hand. Have fun writing them back to front or upside down, in mirror writing, or in various colors and styles—tiny, massive, whatever.

HOW DO YOU FEEL NOW?

Do you feel energized? Was it enjoyable? Or not? It is an exercise that forces you to progress slowly and learn on the job, as if you were a child again. Be patient with yourself. Did you feel less, or more, concentrated on this task? Does it make you want to draw things?

....
....
....
....
....
....
....
....
....
....
....
....
....
....
....
....
....
....
....
....
....
....
....
....

Spontaneous calligraphy

DAY 200

First, find yourself 30 sheets of ordinary printer paper, a calligraphy brush, and some ink. Now, start to trace signs onto the paper that have no actual meaning—you might think of them as an unknown language. The idea is to make the signs while in a really relaxed frame of mind. No need to judge what you are doing, and no need, either, to pay much attention to the pages as they fill up. Concentrate on making the marks quickly and freely, feel the energy running through you, and don't really think about any of it.

Now close your eyes and imagine an intense ray of light coming down from the sun, or some divine being, and it passes through your head and runs through your arm and into your hand, right through to the tip of the brush and the ink, where it dances freely on the page. Now continue to make your signs, fast and fluid.

This can all feel a little chaotic at the start, but that's how it should be. As you work through more pages, your hand will become more supple, and the pleasure will increase. When all the sheets are filled up, leave the exercise without even looking back at what you have done. Reflect on how you feel. Do you sense a particular kind of energy?

WHAT WAS THE EXPERIENCE LIKE FOR YOU?

....
....
....
....
....
....
....
....
....
....
....
....
....

THE NEXT DAY, TAKE A LOOK AT THOSE PAGES.

Look at them closely. Do you see an evolution as you went on? Perhaps a more supple and fluid line? Or repeated signs? Choose the sheets that you like the most, cut them out, and stick them into your creative notebook.

....
....
....
....
....
....
....
....
....
....
....
....
....
....
....

In search of well-being

Prioritizing your own well-being is an ideal way of freeing yourself from overthinking, and all the blockages that come with that. It also helps you accept the situation as it is, rather than thinking only of how you would like it to be. So how can you put well-being first? Meditation is a great way to start, and so is spending time thinking about positive memories that can fill you with a sense of joy and gratitude, an appreciation of your own inner resources. Put yourself first, and let go!

MAKE A LIST OF POSSIBLE ACTIVITIES TO PROMOTE YOUR WELL-BEING. CHOOSE ONE AND DO IT TODAY.

....
....
....
....
....
....
....
....
....
....
....
....

If you are having trouble letting go, just remind yourself that there is nothing at risk here, in these few moments of relaxation. **You may as well have a go!**

....
....
....
....
....
....
....
....
....
....

A ritual for letting go

We can get deeply attached to many things without realizing it. Think about some of your creative projects that you never finished, but that are still lying around somewhere. It can be hard to admit we'd be better off without them—that we could throw them into the trash! They are most likely things you don't want to work on anymore, because you've changed your mind, or your creative focus has shifted. So now is the time to make way for new, fresher, more stimulating ideas.

Write down in a few words the projects you feel ready to part with. No need for explanations, just name them. Then fold the sheet of paper into something—a paper plane, a boat, or simply crumple it up into a ball. Next, you're going to hand over these projects, symbolically speaking, to the universe, where they will be recycled into something else. Perhaps burn a stick of incense to heighten the mood.

WHAT KIND OF RITUAL WOULD YOU LIKE TO CREATE TO LET GO OF ALL THESE? BURN THEM IN A FIRE, MAYBE? PUT THEM IN A SHREDDER?

....
....
....
....
....
....

leave space for your creative energy

Put on some inspiring music and imagine waves of creative energy flowing through your body. Let your body unwind, imagine you are gently dancing as you let go, and feel yourself carried by this creative wave. Imagine the creativity is now in your hands, an expression of all the energy that is running through your body, giving you an exquisite sense of pleasure and joy. How are you feeling now? Do you feel like laughing or singing?

WRITE ABOUT YOUR EXPERIENCE.

About time

DAY
204

How you feel about time

Our relationship with the passing of time can be a complicated one. All of us have the same number of hours in a day, but the difference is in how we manage to use it. So time plays an important role in creativity, and it's best to think of it as an ally, not an enemy. Our perception of time often makes us overestimate what we can achieve in one day. Equally, we often underestimate what we can achieve across a whole year! If you set yourself a target of just 15 minutes a day for a whole year, then you will make real progress in your projects. But our lives are so complex, and even carving out 15 or 30 minutes a day can seem impossible. If that is the case, just stop and consider how much benefit you, personally, can get from spending 15 minutes to recenter and regroup your energy.

Let's now look at how you feel about time. Are you fearful of wasting time? Do you think you don't deserve spending time on yourself? Do you feel guilty if you take time for yourself, and for your creativity? Are you afraid that a creative project will take too much of your time? Do you use lack of time as an excuse for not doing creative things?

WRITE DOWN YOUR RESPONSES, AND DON'T JUDGE YOURSELF!

....
....
....
....
....
....
....
....
....
....
....

How do you spend your time?

Today, I'd like to invite you to look at how much time you put into the various parts of your day. What are the different activities that fill up each of your days? Time spent at work, doing household chores, relaxation, social and family activities, exercise, and of course, sleep. But how about time to create, to learn or discover new things? Make a list of each of your activities, and note throughout the day how much time you are putting into each one, and then make a rough pie chart.

DOES THE RESULT SEEM TO BE BALANCED, OR SKEWED IN ONE DIRECTION? DO SOME ACTIVITIES EAT UP YOUR TIME FOR NO GAIN? ARE YOU MISSING OUT ON ACTIVITIES YOU REALLY ENJOY?

....
....
....
....
....
....
....
....
....
....
....
....
....

For the coming week, do this exercise daily, and write down your observations in your notebook. The idea here is to help you see (without self-judgement) how you tend to spend your time, with the aim of eventually spending more time on the things that are important to you.

> AT THE END OF THE WEEK, DRAW A NEW PIE CHART
> SHOWING WHAT YOU HAVE LEARNED.

Going on strike

Have you ever added up the time you spend watching TV, glued to social media, or browsing the web? Be honest with yourself: is this time really fueling the development of your creative self? Imagine a day with no smartphone, landline, TV, computer, tablet, Internet, book, magazine, or newspaper to see what might happen, and if it might open a new window onto your creativity.

Try giving yourself a day off from technology. If you can't do it today, then plan a day in the future when it suits you, but soon. See it as an enriching experience from which you can learn at the same time.

HOW DO YOU FEEL ABOUT THIS IDEA?

Is part of you resistant to doing this? Do you feel dependent on technology? How could you imagine using the free time that this gives you? And if you have managed to do this already, then congratulations! How was it for you, and what conclusions can you draw from the experience?

....
....
....
....
....
....
....
....
....
....
....
....
....
....
....
....
....
....
....

Balancing your time

Look back over what you have discovered about your use of time over the previous days.
Are you happy with the way you tend to use your time? How could you rebalance your time?
How could you reduce time spent on certain tasks, so you have more time to do the things you
find more beneficial, and more time to be creative?

WRITE DOWN ANYTHING THAT COMES TO MIND,
AND THINK ABOUT HOW YOU COULD PUT THIS INTO ACTION IN YOUR LIFE.

....
....
....
....
....
....
....
....
....
....
....
....
....
....
....
....
....
....
....
....
....
....
....
....
....
....
....

Organizing with creativity

How about organizing your week with a bit of creativity? In this exercise, you are going to make a "Running List," which is a bit like a classic "To Do" list, but which also combines all of your appointments, events, and everything else that is coming up over the week.

On a double page of your notebook, make a list of all the events and appointments for the coming week on the left-hand side, and a list of tasks on the right-hand page. In the space between these two, draw seven vertical columns, one for each day of the week. Each time you complete a task, color in a square in the column corresponding to that day. The list gives you a visual of everything you need to do in the week, as well as everything that's been achieved!

Try out a Bullet Journal®

The Bullet Journal® is a way of organizing tasks and events using a creative notebook. You can be better organized and more productive, while at the same time having a creative way to manage your time. It was created by an American digital product designer, Ryder Carroll, and is summed up in the slogan: "Track the past, organize the present, plan the future." Its advantages are its flexibility, allowing it to be tailored to your own needs!

The Bullet Journal® works with your own creative handwriting and all kinds of icons that you can invent for yourself. Create one icon for each activity, and you can integrate your own ideas into certain parts of the book.

ARE YOU TEMPTED TO GIVE IT A TRY?

....
....
....
....
....
....
....
....
....
....
....
....
....
....

You will find plenty of examples of Bullet Journals® on the Internet, or better still, take a look at Ryder Carroll's website: bulletjournal.com.

Time to review

You have just completed your 30th week of this journey, and well done for coming this far! That's quite some journey already! Can you measure the time you have been able to invest in your own creativity so far? How about using your creative time today simply to get the most out of life? Write down your thoughts here.

....
....
....
....
....
....
....
....
....
....
....

WEEK 31
It's cyclical

Creative cycles

Our creative energy comes from the universe—from life itself. It takes shape within us, working at its own rhythm over the passage of time. Understanding these rhythms helps us get a clearer vision of what lies ahead for us in our creative enterprises, so that we can move forward with confidence. There is a time for everything, and accepting the various phases of the creative cycle provides us with a solid foundation on which to build. For a great example of a creative cycle, we need look no further than the passage of the seasons: just as spring always follows winter, the creative cycles too have their own order and logic.

HAVE YOU NOTICED CYCLICAL PATTERNS IN YOUR OWN LIFE, IN YOUR CREATIVE LIFE, OR IN YOUR CREATIVE PROJECTS?

....
....
....
....
....
....
....
....
....
....
....
....

The cycle of creative energy

As time passes, you'll find that your creative energy follows its own ups and downs, almost as if it needs time to rest and regroup before heading for the next high point. Clarissa Pinkola Estés, author of *The Creative Fire*, provides a particularly enlightening explanation, which forms the basis of the diagram below. I like to think of it more as a spiral than a closed circle.

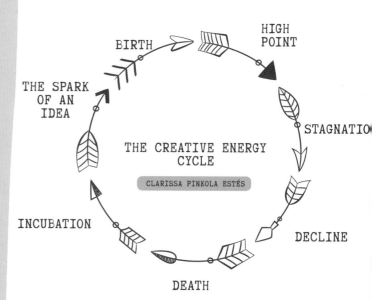

THE CREATIVE ENERGY CYCLE

CLARISSA PINKOLA ESTÉS

BIRTH · HIGH POINT · STAGNATION · DECLINE · DEATH · INCUBATION · THE SPARK OF AN IDEA

Being creative while following this rhythm means being attentive to the changing levels of creative energy during the "downtime": in other words, you can't push hard all the time, in the way that you can't force a plant to grow quickly. Where are you today in your creative energy cycle? Are you in a contemplative stage, or maybe reaping what you sowed some months ago?

....
....
....
....
....
....

Winter

In the creative cycle, winter is a time of rest and regeneration. There is a purpose to it, of course, which is to replenish your inner resources. The work goes on, but unseen, as ideas begin to take shape. Creative energy retreats into itself. It is a time for you to feed your inspiration.

**HOW DO YOU EXPERIENCE THESE CREATIVE "WINTERS"?
DO YOU TRY TO AVOID THEM, RATHER THAN REAP THE BENEFITS?**

....
....
....
....
....
....
....
....
....
....
....
....

Spring

In the creative spring, energy returns, eager to find expression and prompting us to sow our ideas on fertile soil, where some, at least, will take root. It is a powerfully creative time, though the results are not immediately visible and we can feel impatient, waiting for our ideas to take shape.

HOW DO YOU EXPERIENCE THESE TIMES?

Are you impatient to move things along more quickly? Or do you manage to savor every moment of this phase? Do you tend to hold back these surges in creative energy, to resist this interior urge to act and create?

....

....

....

....

....

....

....

....

....

Summer

It's the creative summer, and your ideas are starting to take physical shape. They are flowering, if you will, but will need more time to ripen and produce fruit. This can make us feel doubly impatient, as we yearn for quicker results. Now is the time to rein in that creative energy slightly, making time to pause and think about your actions and plans.

DO YOU GET ADDICTED TO THIS "CREST OF THE WAVE" MOMENT IN THE CREATIVE CYCLE? DO YOU TEND TO PUSH TOO MUCH AT THIS STAGE?

....

....

....

....

....

....

....

....

DAY 216

Fall

With the arrival of fall, it's time to harvest the fruit of our labor. We need to be mindful not to try to bring in the fruit before it's ripe: in other words, not to stop a project too soon in our haste to complete it. You know this "ripe" moment when you see it: the point where there is no need to refine the work anymore, nor to add anything else to it. At the same time, you'll find your creative energy in decline, and you may be trying to fight against that.

**IT IS ALSO TIME TO REVIEW AND CELEBRATE
THE WORK YOU HAVE DONE.
WHAT DID YOU LEARN? WHAT COULD YOU IMPROVE?**

....
....
....
....
....
....
....
....
....
....
....
....

A symbolic act

Today, I'd like you to plant an actual seed to symbolize your creative project and celebrate the creative cycle. You'll need a pot, soil, water, and the seeds themselves—chosen according to the season you're in at the moment.

Think about what you would like to cultivate in your own life. What project, or perhaps what personal quality, would you like to nurture and grow? As you plant the seeds in the pot, think about your personal aims and aspirations. Water it, being mindful of the patience, love, and attention that you will be giving the seeds during their germination. As the green shoots push through the earth, watch them grow as the days pass. This exercise will perhaps help you think about your own project with tenderness and patience, knowing that everything is in place, and that often we can't see what is developing below the surface.

HOW CAN YOU TAKE CARE OF YOUR OWN CREATIVITY?
WHAT KIND OF "FERTILIZER" MIGHT YOU NEED? NOTE DOWN ANY IDEAS.

Keeping to the rhythm

DAY 218

Your biorhythms

Our bodies follow their own rhythms, and by working with these rhythms (rather than against them) we have a better chance of accomplishing our creative goals. By knowing a bit more about biorhythms, we can adapt our activities to this cycle: if you are worn out and short on sleep, you will clearly not be at your most creative!

ARE YOU AWARE OF YOUR OWN RHYTHMS?

Are you more of a morning person or an evening person? Today, watch for fluctuations in your level of energy. Note when you have the most energy, and when you are most productive, or when you need to kick back and take some time out, or when you feel moments of inspiration. Ideally, repeat this over several days or even weeks. At the end of the period, look over your results. Are there any patterns forming?

....
....
....
....
....
....
....
....
....
....
....
....
....
....

DAY
219

Follow your own rhythm

Understanding our own rhythms teaches us to tap into creative energy when it is present.
It's a subtle skill, and requires careful listening to our own bodies and our own motivations.

Try out what works best for you, even if it feels tricky at the start: it is worth the effort.
And remember to be aware of your own needs—for rest, for recreation, or for moments
of intense activity. Can you become aware of when your creative energy is present?

Watch carefully over the coming days to see how your creative project draws you in.
Do you manage to resist working on it because it is time to eat, or time to go to bed?
Or because you are doing something else, perhaps going out with a friend?
Would you ever cancel on someone just because you felt it was more important
to work on your creative project instead?

How could you organize your life to become more attuned to the ebb and flow of
your creative rhythms? Would you, for example, allow yourself to turn down an invitation
from a friend because you are "otherwise engaged" on your creative project?

NOTE DOWN WHAT COMES TO MIND, WITHOUT JUDGING YOURSELF.

....

....

....

....

....

....

....

....

....

....

....

....

....

....

....

....

....

....

A regular practice

DAY 220

Regular practice, without getting stuck in a rigid routine, will help create a powerful rhythm in your creative work.

Try to build some momentum to help maintain your creative work, like a marathon runner, step after step, hour by hour. The amount of energy that you feel able to put into your project will increase as the days go on, and the momentum will drive you on, even when your energy and motivation dip. Establishing this rhythm will carry you beyond what you thought you were capable of. It is like a magic dust that will see you getting better, and moving further, in what you want to achieve. The more you train, the better will be your creative practice, and the more you will have to show for it.

WRITE DOWN YOUR THOUGHTS AND FEELINGS ABOUT THIS.

....
....
....
....
....
....
....
....
....
....
....
....
....
....
....
....
....
....
....
....

Planning your work

HOW ABOUT TRYING TO PLAN YOUR NEXT THREE MONTHS' ACTIVITIES, INCLUDING WORK ON YOUR CREATIVE PROJECTS? USE YOUR DIARY OR CALENDAR TO HELP YOU.

Could you make a detailed plan over the coming months that gives you a daily time slot to work on an important stage of your creative project? Use your diary and see how you can fit this in alongside all your other commitments.

MAKE A FIRM
DECISION TO
KEEP TO IT!
ARE YOU READY?

DAY
222

Test yourself

Choose an important project and make a firm commitment to give it half an hour of your time each day for the coming week: no excuses! At the end of each session, note how you feel and the progress you made (or didn't make). At the week's end, reread your notes.

WHAT DID YOU LEARN?

How did this go? Did you make a load of progress? Or were you frustrated not to get far enough? Did you spot how you try to get around doing the task? What could you do better?

....
....
....
....
....
....
....
....
....
....
....
....

It's okay to break the rhythm

Planning and structure can be a great help. But if the work rhythm becomes a bit too routine and starts taking the pleasure out of what you're doing, then it's time for a rethink.

It's not a setback. Rather, it is a much-needed break so you can pick up again in better shape, with your batteries fully charged. In fact, it is exactly what happened to me as I was writing this book! Feeling a bit under pressure to deliver, I took time out by the ocean for a few days and did some writing in a completely new setting. I could feel the extra creative energy as a result. Have you experienced something like this, where you change your rhythm completely and then reap the benefits? Maybe it was just about working in a different room, or at a different time, or with more time off to rest.
What could you do to soften up your own work rhythms?

NOTE WHAT COMES TO MIND.

....
....
....
....
....
....
....

The rhythm of your heart

Getting into a work rhythm, and sticking to it, is not as constraining as you may think. By making ourselves available to work on it, week in, week out, we're getting closer each time to our own creative source. If it feels like a chore, then it's time to rethink what this project means to you, and whether it still matters.

Take some time to think about what you love about your project. What does it bring you? Do you feel as if you are growing too, as the project advances? Or do you need to make changes? Make a list of what you love about your project, and feel your energy picking up.

WHAT ARE YOU FEELING NOW?

....
....
....
....
....
....
....
....
....
....
....

The present Moment

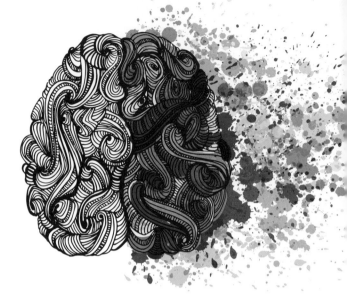

Mental drift

DAY 225

The mind is all too capable of sidestepping our carefully developed creative energy and chucking a whole load of doubts and fears into our path, throwing us off course and distracting us from the things that matter. Suddenly, we are totally distracted by a bunch of negative thoughts. It can happen in a flash! And the only way to try to beat it is to stay focused on the present moment, coming back to the task at hand, because this is where your creative energy will be found.

Today, then, try to stay on high alert against this mental drift. As soon as you feel your mind wandering into unwelcome thoughts, bring yourself back to what you are doing. To help you in this, keep your notebook nearby and mark an "x" on the page every time you notice your mind moving away from your activity, whatever it happens to be. And you can be honest with yourself, as there is nothing to judge here: your mind is just doing what it does!

At the end of the day, review what happened. Were you surprised by the number of crosses that you marked down in your book? Have you tried to observe how you manage to drift out of the present moment? Are you surprised at finding you want to do something else instead? And what does that mean to you?

HOW WAS THIS EXPERIENCE FOR YOU?

....
....
....
....
....
....
....
....
....
....
....
....
....
....
....
....
....

Being present in the creative process

When we are not fully present in the creative process, work becomes a drag, everything feels difficult, we can't figure out how to move forward, we get bored, and we begin to lose interest in what we are doing. Effectively, we are throwing the power switch and turning off that current within us that seeks to express itself in a creative way.

When we are right in the sweet spot of the creative process, everything feels very different. We are concentrated, and can feel that creative energy flowing within us. We feel fulfilled by what we are doing, energized, and somehow guided in what to do next. Time seems to stand still. In fact, we can become so in love with the process itself that the end result becomes less of a deal!

Have you experienced times when you felt disconnected from the creative process and wanted to give up? Or moments when your entire being felt part of the work you were doing? What conclusions did you draw? When you feel disconnected, how can you get back on track?

TALK ABOUT A TIME WHEN YOU FELT COMPLETELY PRESENT IN WHAT YOU WERE DOING (CREATIVE OR NOT). WHAT DID IT FEEL LIKE?

Breathing your way back to the present

DAY 227

A very simple way of coming back to the present moment is to focus on your breathing. In his book *The Power of Now*, Eckhart Tolle writes that becoming fully aware of our breathing has the effect of "dis-identifying" with our mind. This opens the door to a feelings of peace and joy, which are naturally present within us.

Can you become aware of your breathing? And do you ever forget to breathe? When your mind is a bit too worked up, do you ever try to calm yourself down by breathing? For the whole of today, pay attention to your breathing, as often and as carefully as you can.

AT THE END OF THE DAY, NOTE DOWN WHAT YOU HAVE OBSERVED. DID YOU SEE ANY DIFFERENCES?

Back to your senses

DAY 228

I'd like you to put all your attention into thinking about how your body is feeling. As soon as you feel that your mind is starting to wander, take a deep breath and put your body through your mental "scanner," picking up all the sensations that run through your body.

What happened during these moments? Did you feel tension or pain, and if so, what kinds and where? Imagine that you're making an exploration of your body, and note what you're discovering. What colors can you see, what are you hearing, what can you smell?

AT THE END OF THE DAY, WRITE DOWN YOUR OBSERVATIONS. HOW DID IT GO? WHAT DID YOU THINK? DID IT FEEL GOOD?

Come back to the present moment

Some craft activities demand a high level of concentration and are particularly suited to being "in the moment." Kirigami, for example, is a Japanese craft involving precision paper cutting, and requires total concentration (to avoid painful accidents too!), with the benefit of calming your mind and forcing a kind of mental discipline. In practice, it comes very close to meditation. Calligraphy, stained glass work, and even coloring mandalas can create a similar feeling.

So today, how about trying a creative discipline that has this effect of bringing you fully into the present moment? What are you tempted by? Make a space for this activity in your diary, and in the meantime, draw yourself a mandala (see also Day 69) and carefully color it in. Let your breathing settle into a calm rhythm, take plenty of time, and concentrate. After about 15 minutes, see whether you feel calmer inside. How are you feeling now? What, if anything, has changed?

WRITE DOWN YOUR EXPERIENCE HERE.

....
....
....
....
....
....
....
....
....
....

Try something new

Whatever you find yourself doing, there is always a way to bring yourself back to the present moment during your daily life. It takes a bit of effort, but the benefits will make it worthwhile. There are plenty of disciplines to help you with this. Anything that calms the mind will help you bring more mindfulness into what you are doing.

WHAT KINDS OF THINGS HAVE YOU ALREADY TRIED IN THIS AREA? IN YOUR DIARY, PLAN TO TRY OUT A NEW DISCIPLINE, AND DESCRIBE YOUR EXPERIENCE.

....
....
....
....
....
....
....
....
....
....
....
....
....
....
....
....
....
....
....
....
....
....

A practical exercise

Choose a creative activity that you enjoy. The idea here is to try to concentrate as much as you can on the physical aspects, gestures, and movements, rather than the thinking part, and to watch what you do with a sense of curiosity, as if you were discovering the techniques for the first time. Try to involve all your senses in what you are doing. So if you have opted for painting, for example, choose a simple theme or even just a random mix of colors. Concentrate on the texture of the paint and its odor, the sound of the brush on the paper, the movements your hands make: slow everything down, feeling the energy in your arms and hands. If your mind wanders, return to the present, focusing on your breathing. Do this exercise for at least 10 minutes. How do you feel now, and did the feeling change during the exercise?

WRITE DOWN YOUR EXPERIENCES.

....
....
....
....
....
....
....
....
....
....
....
....
....
....
....
....
....
....

Patience

Impatience

Impatience is a kind of dissatisfaction with the present moment. No sooner have we started out, and we want to be finished already. We are so focused on the end result (that we imagine is going to be awesome) that we totally forget about the creative process. All this creates a kind of emotional charge that ramps up the frustration that we can't complete our stuff more quickly. And this vicious circle of frustration and annoyance pushes us to throw ourselves into yet more ambitious projects, with the risk of finishing none of them!

Sounds familiar? How can you manage this tendency that we all have? Are you impatient with your projects? Do you want to finish before you have even begun? Do you get all fired up and then fail to complete? Can you remember this happening with certain projects in particular? What happened, exactly? What did you learn?

NOTE DOWN WHAT COMES TO MIND WHEN YOU READ THESE QUESTIONS.

Swimming against the current

Wanting to go too fast is a bit like swimming against the current. We end up using a lot of creative energy with the aim of realizing an amazing result, and we end up getting nowhere: we become blocked. Deadlines can lead to a sense of urgency that makes us panic. So does a project that seems beyond our capabilities. We get blocked, frustrated, and end up wasting time. In a world where everything seems to be speeding up, patience is no longer a virtue. So it is easy to get discouraged by the slow pace of some of our projects.

Why do you think you sometimes want to go so fast? Suppose you tried to draw this impatient inner self of yours: how would you make it look? Is it like a terrifying monster, or a hyperactive monkey, or something else altogether? Maybe take a look at some cartoon books to get inspiration. Now take a step back from this aspect of yourself, and imagine that you can have a conversation with it.

WHAT WOULD YOU WANT TO SAY?

....
....
....
....
....
....
....
....
....
....
....
....
....
....
....
....
....
....

Ideas need time to mature

Patience is absolutely essential for creativity to take place. We often need to remind ourselves that we live in a material, physical world, and that to make our ideas into something concrete means adapting to the constraints of the world around us. A simple metaphor for this can be drawn from nature: a fruit that has not had time to ripen will not taste good. In the same way, your creative project needs time to mature, slowly but surely. Even if your idea seems crystal clear in your own mind right now, you will still need to give it time to germinate, grow and ripen.

How can you be more patient—and calm—in your own creative work? How about simplifying the process, so you only retain aspects that are most important to you? Alternatively, you could slow everything down, or perhaps lower your expectations of the end result. Do you take regular breaks, and try to do just one thing at a time? How could you get these practices into your life at the moment? What would be a first step?

NOTE DOWN ANY IDEAS ON THIS, AND START TODAY TO PUT THEM INTO ACTION.

Delays

When creative projects slow down, get delayed, or seem to be going nowhere, it can get frustrating. But if life seems to be throwing obstacles onto our creative path, it forces us to stop and think. A delay is sometimes the best thing that can happen, allowing us to rethink something with a new creative vision, rather than just following a list of tasks that might be out of step with the initial idea.

How do you deal with delays? How do you feel about having things slow down, outside of your control? Have you experienced a delay that turned out to be beneficial—perhaps allowing you to find a new, more creative solution? What happened?

DO YOU HAVE A PROJECT THAT GOT DELAYED? HOW DID YOU MANAGE TO BENEFIT FROM THIS DELAY TO THE PROGRAM? NOTE DOWN WHAT HAPPENED.

....
....
....
....
....
....
....
....
....
....

Take your time

Patience is the antidote to getting worked up. It gets us to take our time to be creative, to be in the present moment. It invites us to stop running and start living the creative process to the fullest. For that, we have to allow ourselves to slow down.

Here's an experiment. Take a piece of fruit, wash it, and eat it really, really slowly, as though it were something rare and precious. Try to concentrate on everything about it: how it feels in your hand, its odor, the sensation on your teeth.

Did you notice how the flavors seemed to explode in your mouth? What was the experience like? Was it easy? Or perhaps frustrating and difficult?

NOW TRY TO PUSH THIS EXERCISE EVEN FURTHER, DRAWING OUT ANOTHER ACTIVITY AS SLOWLY AS POSSIBLE. WRITE ABOUT THE EXPERIENCE.

....
....
....
....
....
....
....
....
....

Slow coloring

DAY 237

Coloring is a great exercise in concentration, especially when done slowly! Take a pencil and, on a sheet of paper, draw (as slowly as you can) some geometric outlines, or abstracts, or florals, whatever. The main thing is to draw with all your concentration, being present in the moment, feeling the contact between pencil and paper. Now spend time coloring what you have drawn. How did that go? Did you manage to do everything slowly? Or did you find yourself racing ahead to finish the job? What things did you observe by doing this exercise slowly? Did you see a change in your mood? Did you enjoy it?

WRITE ABOUT YOUR EXPERIENCE.

....
....
....
....
....
....
....
....
....
....

Review time

DAY 238

Congratulations! You have reached the end of this week all about patience. Nice work! **I'd like you now to read back over your notes and see what conclusions you might draw. What did you learn during the week? Has it changed anything for you? Has your view of patience—and slowness—changed over the week? Has it given you any new ideas? What steps could you take to move more in this direction? What would be the first step?**

NOTE DOWN ANY THOUGHTS THAT COME TO YOU.

Learn to navigate

Staying on course

It's not at all unusual to lose all sense of direction in a creative project. We can get so tied down in the daily routine, and in the creative process itself, that we can sometimes find ourselves suddenly stuck, with no idea how to figure out the next step. The remedy for this is to return as regularly as possible to the things that are most important to us: our values and the "whys" that lie behind the project itself. By keeping a clear vision of what the project is for, you will be able to keep a firm sense of where you are and plot your course through to your destination, whatever comes at you on the way.

HOW DO YOU REACT WHEN YOU HIT A PROBLEM?

Do you check where you're at with your creative projects regularly enough? Take a moment to redefine what is really at the heart of one of the projects you are working on right now. What is important to you about this project? Reread the list you made on Day 75, and use it as a starting point to make a new list of "Why?" questions: 30 reasons why your project matters to you. That may seem like a lot to ask, but doing this can kick-start your motivation and give you a clearer vision of your aims.

Learn to surf

Imagine you just had an amazing idea. And you know exactly how your project is going to turn out, and how you're going to make it happen. Except that nothing is going to plan! So much the better. Because when things go against you, the creative process is at its best, demanding that you use all of your flexibility to adapt to whatever the project throws back at you. The best time to be creative is when we have to adjust our creative energies to deal with problems, slowdowns, peaks, and troughs. This approach teaches us to make the best of what we have in front of us, and to go with the mood that we're in and the energy we have at the time. It is about swimming *with* the current, rather than against it, having confidence in our intuition that it will take us in the right direction.

Have you experienced moments like this, where you have been able to adjust to what lies before you? How did it feel? Recount what this was like for you, and how you dealt with the point where the wave ran out of energy. Have you experienced huge slowdowns in your work, when everything seemed to fall into a chasm? And did that teach you something about yourself too?

NOTE DOWN ANY THOUGHTS THAT INSPIRE YOU.

....
....
....
....
....
....
....
....
....
....
....
....
....
....
....
....
....

A neat trick

It can be helpful to have several projects in the works at the same time. Obviously, we don't want to spread our creativity too thinly with too many, but having two or three in progress simultaneously means it is easier to put one aside when you feel the energy is simply not there, and work on some of the others. In a sense, you're following the path of least resistance, and this is no bad thing: you are listening for which of your projects suits you the best at any given time.

Which creative project are you working on at the moment? Do you have another project that you can work on in parallel? Do you see ways in which the two are complementary? Perhaps working on one is feeding in creatively to the other? If you don't have a second project on stream, could you start one?

MAKE A LIST OF POSSIBILITIES.

....
....
....
....
....
....
....
....
....
....
....
....
....
....
....
....
....
....
....
....

React, don't think!

Another quality that comes in useful as you try to navigate your way through a project is the ability to react quickly, without overthinking. As we start out on any project, we can be caught up in a lot of emotional hang-ups, and the smallest setback can be extremely dispiriting and feel like a catastrophe, leaving us unsure where to go next and asking ourselves questions like "Why did that happen to me?" The solution to this is essentially to keep moving, to keep the momentum of the project going, and to react, rather than reflect.

Make a list of 20 things that you could do straight away, which you would like to do and which you really enjoy.

Choose one of these, and do it right now. No need to spend any time thinking: just get started!

WRITE DOWN YOUR IDEAS.

....
....
....
....
....
....
....
....
....
....
....
....
....
....

Navigating the storms

The difficulties we face can be seen as a crucial guide to our level of creative resources: like the fuel gauge in our car. The better we are at reading what these setbacks are telling us, the better we will be at responding to them freely and calmly, rather than panicking. It takes a certain amount of self-belief to do this, because the meaning of what's going on may only emerge further down the line. The next step you take may turn out to be in the wrong direction, but that is okay too: you are learning and growing from the process.

How do you deal when your project runs into stormy weather? Do you stay positive and remain optimistic? Do you see the crisis as an opportunity, providing you with benefits that have yet to be revealed?

NOTE DOWN ANY THOUGHTS INSPIRED BY THIS APPROACH

....
....
....
....
....
....
....
....
....
....
....
....

Put up with some temporary discomfort

Being driven by our creative energy is not always a comfortable feeling. While there can be some awesome moments where everything seems to flow, at other times it can feel quite brutal, making us question what we're doing. But here's the thing: the more we accept that there will be setbacks and problems, the less energy we waste fighting against them, thus keeping our minds freer and more relaxed. Of course, we have to figure out what kind of approach suits us best. But the more we push back against the inevitable setbacks that come our way, the further we are from recovering our creative energy.

Have you experienced times in your creative life that have felt uncomfortable? How do you feel about them now? And what could you do today to deal a little better with moments like this?

NOTE DOWN ANY IDEAS THAT COME UP.

....
....
....
....
....
....
....
....
....
....
....
....
....
....
....
....
....
....

Let yourself go

Take a deep breath and exhale slowly. Put on some soft, inspirational music, and let your thoughts and feelings bubble up to the surface. Think about how relaxation can allow you to be at one with the cycle of your own creativity. By letting go, by not swimming against the current, you can let yourself be carried gently down into a wave, before the wave carries you up once more. At the crest of that wave, pause to appreciate the awesome moment, giving complete meaning to your creative endeavors and spurring you to go yet further. You know that these moments do not last forever, but also that there will be others to come. Knowing all this can put you in a state of relaxation where you are open to all of life's surprises: the unexpected phone call that suddenly gets you past a creative block; a book picked up at random that seems to be calling to you; a conversation with a friend… All are signs that the whole of life itself is with you on your creative journey.

HAVE YOU ALREADY EXPERIENCED SURPRISE MOMENTS LIKE THIS THAT HAVE HELPED YOU GET BEYOND A CREATIVE BLOCK? WRITE THEM DOWN—THEY ARE RARE AND PRECIOUS.

LIE DOWN AND TAKE A DEEP BREATH. CLOSE YOUR EYES AND IMAGINE THAT YOU ARE FLOATING ON AN OCEAN OF CREATIVITY, AND YOUR WHOLE BODY FEELS RELAXED AND AT PEACE. LET YOURSELF GO, AND ENJOY THE MOMENT.

Creativity and mindfulness

This week, you have a series of exercises designed to build a sense of your own presence within your creativity. The idea is to build up your ability to stay focused on the present moment—to be mindful, if you will—and to put all other thoughts to one side. Take time to work on each exercise as slowly as possible, in a place where you won't be disturbed. The exercises are designed to be simple, allowing you to forget about results and concentrate purely on the creative process and how it feels in the moment.

DAY 246

Egg-based painting

Take a moment to get yourself focused. Now prepare the painting mixtures, first breaking an egg and separating out the yolk, and then dividing it among a few small cups. In each cup, add some spices or other ingredients to create colors: for example, paprika for red, cocoa for brown hues, beet juice, and so on. Test out and adjust each color on some thick drawing paper. Stay focused on these color mixes, then take a clean sheet of paper and draw some patterns—whatever comes to mind. Apply the paint slowly, taking note of every sensation, from the odor of the spices to the sound of the brush sweeping the paper.

**How was this for you? Did you enjoy the slowness? What were you feeling?
Don't judge yourself harshly if it did not feel as good as you expected.
You did your best. And it can be really hard to slow down when
we have spent our lives doing everything quickly.
What could you do to enjoy this kind of exercise more?**

WRITE DOWN WHATEVER COMES TO MIND.

....
....
....
....
....
....
....
....
....

A bit more time with your inner child

Breathe gently, close your eyes, and call to mind your inner child. Imagine they are sitting opposite you. Look carefully at the scene: where are you? How are they doing? Take time to talk to them, and show that you care for them. Try to be totally present for them, and see how this feels for you. What would they like to do with you today—and what would you like to do for them? Imagine giving them a gift, and then talk together, trying to stay as close as possible to yourself and to them, letting yourself be carried along by the scene. When you feel like it, open your eyes and come back to yourself. Write down what happened, and how you felt about the quality of presence that you were able to experience.

HOW DID YOU FEEL?

....
....
....
....
....
....
....
....
....
....
....
....
....
....
....
....
....
....
....
....
....

The bigger picture

Take a moment to settle yourself. Breathe gently and close your eyes, and try to be as fully in the present moment as you can. Now take a picture from your creative happy box or cut one from a magazine. Stick it on the center of a piece of drawing paper, and look closely at the image. What does it inspire in you? Now start by extending some of the lines from the image onto the drawing paper, and try to imagine what takes place beyond the limits of the image itself. Listen closely to your intuition, your ideas and desires, without judging, filtering, or censoring in any way. Just focus on the image in front of you and let your imagination run free.

How did you find this exercise? Was anything about it difficult? Were you surprised to find that you were judging yourself? Did you manage to stay in the moment? How did you feel afterward? How could you be even more present?

NOTE YOUR CONCLUSIONS.

....
....
....
....
....
....
....
....
....
....
....
....
....
....
....
....
....
....
....

In the style of ...

Even if drawing is not really your thing, have a go at this exercise. You may love it!

Choose an artist whose work you like—or a style of drawing or painting that you enjoy. Find a picture in this style of art, and look at it carefully. Think about the techniques that have been used, how the lines were made, how the colors were applied, and how they sit alongside each other. Try to imagine how the artist went about making this particular image, and then try to absorb the artist's state of mind. When you're ready, get your own art materials together, ideally similar kinds to those used in the picture you chose. Now select something from your surroundings (like a coffee cup or a vase of flowers) and make a picture in the same style.

ATTACH A PHOTO OF YOUR PICTURE HERE

WHEN YOU HAVE FINISHED, TAKE A PICTURE OF YOUR COMPOSITION AND STICK IT INTO THIS BOOK.

WHAT WAS THIS EXERCISE LIKE FOR YOU? DID YOU KEEP YOUR CONCENTRATION? DID YOU END UP JUDGING YOURSELF? WHAT DID YOU LEARN FROM THE EXPERIENCE?

....
....
....
....
....
....
....
....
....

Your creative project

How about using today to do some work on your own project, trying to do this as mindfully as you can? Start out by taking a deep breath and pledging to stay in the present moment as much as possible, with all your attention sharply focused on the project at hand.

WHAT WAS IT LIKE FOR YOU? DID YOU FEEL A DIFFERENCE IN THE QUALITY OF YOUR PRESENCE, THANKS TO THE EXERCISES YOU HAVE DONE OVER THE PREVIOUS DAYS? DID YOU LOSE CONCENTRATION? WRITE DOWN YOUR THOUGHTS—AND DON'T JUDGE YOURSELF!

....
....
....
....
....
....
....
....
....
....
....

Harvest time

If you can, try to get out of the house for a walk— maybe to a park or forest, or down by a river, or by the sea. You could take your family or friends, too. Before heading out, try to center yourself using whatever technique you prefer, and concentrate on your breathing and on the rest of your body and every one of your senses. Try to be really in the moment on this walk, so you notice everything, gathering up (with friends or family if they are with you) a whole range of beautiful natural things: twigs, leaves, flowers, pebbles, shells, feathers. Then, find a spot to sit down, surrounded by nature, and draw a mandala. Take a picture of your mandala and stick it into your book.

WHAT WAS THE EXPERIENCE LIKE?
WHAT DID YOU FEEL? WHAT DID YOU DISCOVER?

....
....
....
....
....
....
....
....
....
....
....
....
....
....

Review day

This concludes a week of work on mindfulness, developing your capacity of being fully present in the moment. Congratulations on getting this far!

Now take a moment to read back over your notes on the various exercises and experiences of the past week. What conclusions can you draw? What did you think of these exercises? Did you discover anything about yourself and how you operate? Did you enjoy the idea of doing things more slowly, to a different rhythm? Did you get frustrated? If so, when was that? Have you seen any progress as the week went on? Do you want to work more on this area?

WHAT'S YOUR CONCLUSION ABOUT THE WORK THIS WEEK?

....
....
....
....
....
....
....
....
....
....
....
....
....
....
....
....
....
....
....
....
....
....
....
....

A sense of security

Come out of your shell

DAY 253

All of us develop some kind of protective layer around ourselves to give us a sense of security and to fend off some of the hurtful stuff that life throws at us. But sometimes we can carry this protective shell around with us even when it is no longer needed, with the effect that we get disconnected from our feelings and emotions. The problem is that feelings and emotions (which admittedly can be uncomfortable at times) are also the lifeblood of creativity. Accepting our vulnerability and letting in the emotions may feel risky at first, but in the long run it makes us stronger and more alive.

What does security mean to you? Have you needed to protect yourself in the past? Have you lived through times of great vulnerability—especially in the creative field? What was that like for you? Do you feel you can accept your vulnerability?

Take a sheet of drawing paper and sketch out an image representing one of your protective shells. Then take a pair of scissors to cut out the shell, then cut it up into small pieces. On a second sheet of paper, stick the pieces on as if they represent rocks on the ground, and then take a green pen and draw grass and vegetation growing up and around all these pieces.

WHAT WAS IT LIKE FOR YOU DOING THIS EXERCISE?

....
....
....
....
....
....
....
....
....
....
....
....
....
....
....
....
....
....
....
....
....

Your sense of security

It is not so easy to let creativity run wild if we live our lives with a sense of slight unease. A sense of security is key. It starts with a space where you can feel good and really be yourself. It could be in a spare room, or at the kitchen table, or sitting in bed. Where do you feel comfortable enough to be creative? However, it's not just about the location, and even in a quiet place we can still feel ill at ease. The following exercise will help you reinforce your sense of security. It's about encouraging a sense of well-being and serenity that comes from within you, giving you the confidence to go create!

Take a large sheet of drawing paper and some pencils or markers. Draw the outline of a house, symbolizing both protection and a living space. Keep the lines simple. Draw a figure representing you within the house, and then write in some words around your figure evoking the things that you feel should be protected: perhaps certain emotions and sentiments, the names of people important to you, everything that has value for you. Have fun decorating the picture, or adding collage, and take your time, so you can let this idea of security and protection sink into your consciousness. Stick the drawing into your notebook or attach it to the wall of your house where you will see it frequently. What was this exercise like for you?

HOW DO YOU FEEL NOW?

....
....
....
....
....
....
....
....
....
....
....
....
....
....

Make your own protective bubble

This exercise will allow you to reinforce your sense of security. Close your eyes and concentrate on your heartbeat. Visualize yourself inside a large bubble of a beautiful rose gold tint. You have as much space as you need and can create whatever you want to create. The bubble is supple, but also very strong. It will only allow positive energy to pass through it. Take a moment to fill the bubble with love, goodwill, and tenderness, and feel your body basking in these feelings as they flow through you. Open your eyes. Now, do some drawing, writing, or collage in the space below.

WHAT WAS YOUR EXPERIENCE LIKE?

....
....
....
....
....
....
....
....
....

Protecting the creative process

Some stages of the creative process can leave your ideas a bit exposed, and at these times you need to take care to protect both yourself and your ideas. You don't need to lock up all your ideas in a safe. But you do need to remember that sharing an idea too early can damage it—sapping its energy and originality, or sowing seeds of doubt from someone else's comment or even just a skeptical look. Some ideas need time to get going, staying inside you while they pick up strength. If you start to have doubts and stop believing in your ideas, it will take an enormous amount of energy to return to them and put the project back on track. So be careful whom you share your ideas with. If you do so too early, to the wrong person, you may regret it. Not that it's their fault, it's just that some ideas deserve patience as they mature and pick up momentum and need to be more in shape before being talked about.

DOES THIS RESONATE WITH YOUR OWN EXPERIENCE?

Have you seen one of your ideas killed off before it even got started? What are your current projects, and what stage are they at? Do you need to protect some of these ideas, and if so, how would you do that?

You could put your projects into your protective bubble. Take a sheet of paper and in just a few words describe each of your projects, or simply an idea.
Then take a pink pencil and draw a circle around it all,
as if it were offering magical protection.

....
....
....
....
....
....
....
....
....
....
....
....

Creative visualization

Lie down, close your eyes, and call to mind your inner child. Ask them what could make them feel totally secure. If there were a kind of safe, serene cocoon for them to inhabit, what would it look like? What else would they like? Do they have friends? What do they like doing? Let your imagination run, and when ready, note down your thoughts.

Keeping in mind the ideas that you had about this life for your inner child, try to find some images that correspond with your ideas and create a vision board (see also Day 65). Take a picture of the board and attach it below.

Protecting your heart and soul

Developing a sense of self-love will bring you stability and protection. Take a deep breath, and exhale slowly. Imagine you're being enclosed in your own love, which is all around you like a big warm hug. Now draw a figure that represents your creative self, in the center of a sheet of drawing paper. Then, following the contours of your drawing, write down (using different colors) a series of words describing things you love the most. Using all these words, you're going to create a protective bubble built from your own love and passions that will surround the figure of yourself, spiraling out as you add layer upon layer of writing.

WHAT WAS THAT LIKE FOR YOU?

....
....
....
....
....
....
....
....
....

Make a resource space

Put on some soft and inspiring music, lie down, and close your eyes. Breathe deeply. Imagine that you are flying through the air, over the oceans, feeling weightless and happy. After a while, you see land ahead of you. What does it look like? You slow down and prepare to land. That's it, now you have arrived, and are in the most beautiful landscape you have ever seen. You feel serene and safe.

Could you describe this amazing landscape? Try to remember everything about it. What inspires you about this place? Imagine being in such a perfectly serene state of creative security that you could create anything you wanted to. What would that change for you? What would you dare to do?

Now imagine that you are about to start some new projects, and dream a little about these new ideas. When you feel ready, come back to yourself and write down the feelings this place has evoked in you. Could you find a photograph of a landscape like the one you were imagining? Place it somewhere you can see it. And whenever you feel the need, return to this place in your imagination: it is yours, and only yours.

....
....
....
....
....
....
....
....
....
....
....
....
....
....
....
....

Identifying *your needs*

What are your needs?

DAY 260

We all have needs that our bodies are constantly telling us about. But what exactly is a "need"? According to the dictionary, it's something necessary to life: food, water, sleep … something vital to existence. While biological requirements are easy enough to spot, others are more subtle. The psychologist Abraham Maslow came up with the "Hierarchy of Needs." As well as the basic needs, he added others, such as the need for security. Maslow believed that if our basic needs were not satisfied, we would never be able to meet our needs higher up the order.

Clayton Alderfer further developed Maslow's theories to make a three-way division of needs into categories he called Existence, Relatedness, and Growth (or ERG for short). Here is a summary:

• **Existence needs:** physiological and security needs

• **Relatedness needs:** social and status desires

• **Growth needs:** self-esteem and personal development

How do you think about your own needs? Do you recognize yourself in these classifications? Can you easily identify your needs? Which seem the most important? Today, take time to ask these questions and focus on your needs: do you manage to satisfy them easily? What are your needs at the moment?

NOTE DOWN YOUR THOUGHTS ON THIS DURING THE COURSE OF THE DAY.

SELF-
ACTUALIZATION

SELF-ESTEEM

SOCIAL BELONGING

SECURITY AND PROTECTION

PHYSIOLOGICAL NEEDS

STARTING FROM THE BASE:

• LEVEL 1. PHYSIOLOGICAL NEEDS:
  FOOD—WATER—SLEEP—SHELTER—SEXUALITY

• LEVEL 2. SECURITY AND PROTECTION:
  PERSONAL SECURITY—EMOTIONAL SECURITY—
  FINANCIAL SECURITY—HEALTH

• LEVEL 3. SOCIAL BELONGING:
  FRIENDSHIPS—INTIMACY—FAMILY—COMMUNITY

• LEVEL 4. SELF-ESTEEM: RECOGNITION—
  RESPECT—SELF-CONFIDENCE—INDEPENDENCE

• LEVEL 5. SELF-ACTUALIZATION: REALIZATION
  OF GOALS—HAVING MEANING IN LIFE

....
....
....
....
....
....
....
....
....

Make your own list

Knowing how to be aware of our own needs and to respond to them allows creativity to come more naturally to us. We have all kinds of needs, of course, some of which are easier to spot than others. Start out by making a list and noting down as many of your needs as you can, whatever comes into your mind, no matter how ridiculous they may appear. Take your time, and complete the list as more ideas come up.

....
....
....
....
....
....
....
....
....
....
....
....
....
....

At the end of the day, look through your list and mark the needs that seem to be the most important to you. Remember this is a very personal choice: your priorities are rarely those of someone else. So which are your most important needs, and are they being met? Now make a new list of these "priority" needs, and perhaps put the list into your creative happy box, or leave a copy by your notebook or wallet.

....
....
....
....
....
....

Needs we can't spot

We all have needs that are easy to spot, and many others that are more difficult to identify—and to satisfy. Sometimes, we can feel something is not quite right in our lives, like there is something missing, but without being able to find the right word to describe it or the right way to make it happen. Instead, we might turn to food, TV, the gym, computer games, or drinking to take our minds off this nagging inner voice calling for help. But the irritation does not go away.

Does that evoke anything in your own experience? Do you feel something is missing in your own life? To help think this through, read back over your list and try to sense what it stirs up in you. Often, our first sense of "need" may hide another just behind it: if you're feeling hungry, for example, is it really because you need food, or is there some other desire that is not being met?

So try to listen for your needs in the most profound way you can. Satisfying these more subtle needs takes patience, but it pays off. And staying in the moment, and quietening your mind, will help too.

WHAT DO YOU NEED AT THIS PRECISE MOMENT IN YOUR LIFE?

....
....
....
....
....
....
....
....
....
....
....
....
....
....
....
....

Using creativity to meet your needs

Take another look at the list of needs that you identified. Which ones do you feel are being the most neglected at the moment, and which need attention? Now select between one and three different needs (depending on how complex they are) and think about various ways you could deal with each of them. Be creative, and even if you feel your ideas are totally unrealistic, write down whatever comes to mind. Give yourself enough time, and the ideas will come. You're not looking for a "right" answer here: it's more about being open to whatever comes up. How do you feel about each option? Is there one that is especially appealing?

HOW ABOUT ACTING RIGHT NOW TO MEET ONE OF THESE NEEDS? WHAT WILL YOU DO?

....
....
....
....
....
....
....
....
....
....
....

Our creative needs

Listening to our creative needs can lead us in a number of directions: we could find ourselves in a kind of rest period, able to wait it out patiently and feel our ideas coming together, or it can throw us into an intense period of actively creating, where we seem to have boundless energy to work.

WHERE DO YOU THINK YOU ARE WITH YOUR OWN CREATIVE NEEDS?

How could you express those needs? Sometimes, it is enough simply to cook up a new recipe, or take a photo of your kids, sing in the shower to allow some of those creative needs to be expressed. And what are your creative needs that relate to the project you are working on at the moment? How can those be met?

....
....
....
....
....
....
....

Finding your balance

We're going to look at how your various needs are balanced within different aspects of your life. In the diagram, color the segments according to how you feel you're meeting your needs. (A high rating means you color all the bands to the outer edge. A low-ish score, and you color just the first few bands near the center.)

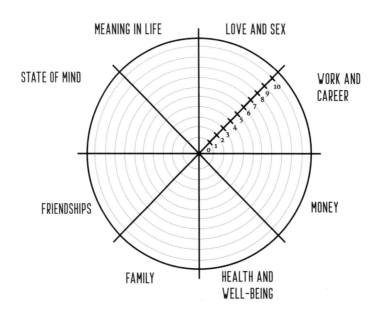

HOW BALANCED ARE ALL THESE PARTS OF YOUR LIFE?

Are there some aspects of your life that seem to be neglected, and how can you meet these needs? Some of these areas are closely linked: to improve your state of mind, you may also need to sleep better or to find a better sense of meaning in the life you lead. What initial step could you make to respond to some of these needs in a creative way?

....
....
....
....
....
....
....
....

PERHAPS YOU'D LIKE TO MAKE ANOTHER COBWEB DIAGRAM, WITH A DIFFERENT SET OF THEMES. WHY NOT DRAW ONE NOW?

Needs of the heart

If we can get to the heart of what it is that we really need, and satisfy those needs, then we are going to create a base from which our creativity will flourish. So listening for those needs, and trying to identify them, is an essential starting point for some of our best creative work.

Lie down comfortably and close your eyes. Place your hands on your heart, and feel its steady beat. As you meditate, ask your heart to guide you to find your equilibrium, and to respond to all your needs. Let your mind run free.

WHEN YOU FEEL READY, COME BACK TO YOURSELF AND NOTE DOWN ANYTHING THAT COMES TO MIND.

....
....
....
....
....
....
....
....
....
....
....
....
....

Taking care of yourself

Listening to yourself

DAY 267

Taking care of ourselves means knowing how to listen to ourselves, to what lies within us and what needs to get expressed. Even if we don't always like what we find on the inside, we have to accept that it's there. Only then can we start to change things.

Do you manage to listen to yourself and get a sense of your interior world? How do you respond when you feel tired or totally stressed out? Do you seek to get away from these feelings as fast as you can? Or do you manage to stand back and think about your feelings? Do you allow time to reconnect with yourself, to get back on track? How can you best take care of yourself? Write down a few notes below.

....
....
....
....
....
....
....
....
....
....
....
....
....

Listening to your body

DAY 268

Creativity is embodied in our physical being, in the sense that our physical bodies are our primary creative tool to express our ideas. So it's time to show some gratitude to our bodies, which allow us to live out our creativity. We can show our appreciation simply by showing love to our bodies, and taking care of them.

HOW DO YOU TAKE CARE OF YOUR BODY?

Lie down, relax, and take a deep breath. Imagine you are putting your body through your mental "scanner." Start at your feet and move slowly up the length of your legs, torso, and arms, through to your head. Can you spot areas of tension or pain? Can you relax even more? Ask yourself how you could take even more care of your body, thinking of sleep, the food you eat, exercise. Should you go to bed earlier? Maybe exercise more? Or take more time for yourself? What more could you do to really care for this amazing body of yours?

....
....
....
....
....
....

Now take a large sheet of drawing paper. Draw the outline of your body, and feel the connection that you have with your physical state. Color in the parts that feel a little tense. Take time to visualize what you are feeling, and express it in your drawing. **How can you represent pain in your drawing? By scribbles? Crosshatching? Color in areas that feel calm.**

WHAT IS IT LIKE TO DO THAT?

....
....
....
....
....
....

How do you treat yourself?

Without realizing it, we actually treat ourselves pretty harshly by refusing to listen to signals of fatigue or tension that our bodies are sending out to us. We need to learn how to understand these warning signals and treat ourselves with a little more kindness and respect, both mentally and physically, thereby reinforcing our sense of worth.

How do you look after yourself? How do you meet your own needs? Do you listen to your needs, or do you tend to ignore them? Do you tend to push yourself beyond your limits?

Do you have ways to pick yourself up when you need to? What kinds of things work for you? Make a list of those simple pleasures that help you build back your inner resources.

CHOOSE ONE OF THESE, AND DO IT NOW!

Learn to keep an eye on your well-being

We can often be quite harsh with ourselves, demanding more and more creativity, better ideas, a higher quality of finish—without realizing that these demands can ultimately be harmful. If you do find that you can sometimes be harsh with yourself, how about trying a softer and more caring route? What do you think of this idea? Perhaps you are already looking after yourself in this way. If so, how?

Sit down and write yourself a letter that is full of encouragement. Recognize that you're doing the best you can, that none of us is perfect, and that you are on a journey that goes at your own pace. What else would you like to add?

WHAT WAS THAT LIKE? WRITE DOWN YOUR THOUGHTS.

....
....
....
....
....
....
....
....
....
....
....
....
....
....
....
....
....

And not forgetting your inner child ...

Taking care of yourself also means taking care of your inner child. Close your eyes and think about your inner child. What kind of warmth and care can you provide for them today? When you were small, what was your favorite meal? How about cooking it (or buying it) right now? Take time to really savor the meal, in the spirit of your younger self.

HOW WAS THIS MOMENT FOR YOU? DID IT FEEL GOOD? WANT TO DO IT AGAIN?

....
....
....
....
....
....
....
....
....
....
....
....
....

Cocooning

Imagine something extremely light and soft, like a silk scarf, something that seems to embody the very essence of "softness." Now get comfortable, slow your breathing, close your eyes, and imagine, in as much detail as you possibly can, that you can wrap yourself in this layer of softness, which is going to nourish you with gentleness throughout your entire body. And now make a promise that you will treat yourself with this kind of gentleness across all aspects of your life: and start to say goodbye to that constant inner critic.

HOW DO YOU FEEL NOW? WHAT WAS IT LIKE TO EXPERIENCE THIS? WRITE DOWN WHAT COMES TO MIND.

....
....
....
....
....
....
....
....
....
....
....
....

YOU CAN
DO THIS EXERCISE AGAIN,
ANY TIME YOU FEEL THE NEED FOR SOME
COMFORT.

Taking care of your creative self

Taking care of ourselves also means accepting all of our imperfections in our creative lives, because they allow us to learn and grow. It means understanding that we are doing our best, whatever the results. It means giving ourselves a second chance, and a third chance, and a fourth. It means recognizing progress, and encouraging ourselves in the face of doubt. Taking care of our creative selves is like a parent who lovingly watches their child learn and grow.

HOW COULD YOU BECOME LIKE A LOVING PARENT TO YOURSELF, AS YOU GROW CREATIVELY? WHAT FIRST STEP COULD YOU MAKE?

....
....
....
....
....

Make a list of your projects. Which ones do you really care about? Which ones would you be ready to give up? Which projects have you put to one side but would like to pick up and work on again, giving them a second chance? And how would you do this?

NOTE DOWN WHAT COMES TO MIND.

....
....
....
....
....
....

DO YOU SEE YOURSELF MAKING PROGRESS SINCE STARTING THIS BOOK? LOOK BACK AT THE JOURNEY YOU HAVE MADE SO FAR. NOTE DOWN ANY THOUGHTS AT THIS TIME.

....
....
....
....
....
....
....

Emotions

Accepting your emotions

As human beings, we live with our emotions. An emotion, then, is a reaction—both physiological and psychological—to a situation we find ourselves in, or the thoughts that we have. Our emotions provide us with a constant measure of our internal state, and they can also show us to what extent our needs are being met—or not. Living our emotions to the fullest can be a frightening experience, sometimes leaving us feeling overwhelmed and shaken up. But the more we try to resist our emotions, the more they can become negative and disruptive to our lives. And in our creative lives, trying to control our emotions can lead to rigidity and blockages. Keeping emotions back means they can build up, eventually bursting through uncontrollably or appearing in the form of physical illness. So learning to accept our emotions is important.

HOW DO YOU LIVE WITH YOUR EMOTIONS?

Do you take the time to listen to your own emotions? Do you recognize what they are? Do you welcome them, and accept them easily? Do you take responsibility for your emotions?

....
....
....
....
....
....

Make a list of the most common emotions that you have experienced during your life. During the coming day, take time to listen to the emotions that you encounter within yourself. Is there one dominant emotion? Write down what you feel today.

....
....
....
....
....
....

Sending a message

Emotions can be unsettling. Often, our first reaction can be to suppress them. We would prefer to dodge our emotions, and there are plenty of ways of doing this: eating too much, binge-watching TV shows, addictions of all kinds. It takes guts to live with, and through, our emotions, but there is a lot to gain from doing so. It is a major step in realizing that something within us is asking for recognition—seeking to break through into our conscious world. When you feel an emotion emerging, try asking yourself: "What is going on here: what message is this sending me?"

Think back to a time when you were struggling to deal with a difficult emotion. Holding that thought, call to mind the protective bubble we talked about on Day 255. Maybe rework that exercise to create a secure space around you. Take your time, surround yourself with your own self-love, and call to mind that difficult emotion. If you feel like crying, let the tears come. Be gentle with yourself. Place your hands over your heart, and ask the emotion what it's trying to tell you. Let any images, thoughts, and ideas bubble up, without holding anything back. And if nothing emerges, just breathe gently and relax, letting yourself go. When you're ready, come back to yourself.

HOW WAS THIS FOR YOU? WHAT DID YOU FEEL AND EXPERIENCE?

....
....
....
....
....
....
....
....
....
....
....
....
....

Writing to transform an emotion

When we are anxious, tired, stressed, or irritable, we're not very creative! There is nothing wrong with being angry or sad, even if these feelings are unpleasant. But to stay in these states for too long can become a problem. And if we then attack ourselves for being in any particular emotional state, we are not solving anything. The good news, however, is that we can use our own creativity to get us feeling better. The idea is to get started on creative activity right away, rather than waiting to feel "better" before we start.

Are you encountering some difficult emotions in your life at the moment? Writing stuff down is a great way to change the direction of your emotions. How about writing a story about someone who is also living with these emotions? What do they do to get through them, or transform them? Take some time to imagine what happens, and write the story in your notebook.

HOW DID THAT GO? AND HOW ARE YOU FEELING NOW? HAS THIS GIVEN YOU SOME IDEAS? NOTE THEM DOWN.

When it comes to writing, you can also use the "morning pages" idea from Julia Cameron that we discussed on Day 64. Because this is something that nobody else is permitted to read, it is a secure place to try to put down your emotions in writing.

....
....
....
....
....
....
....
....
....
....
....
....

Anger and creativity

Anger can sometimes feel like an accumulation of frustrations. It is also full of high-octane emotional energy looking for an outlet, which we can channel into our creative projects.

Is there something that has made you angry recently? What was it? Write it down in a few words, using big letters. Now take your pen and scribble all over the words, destroying what you wrote—and maybe even the paper it's written on! If you want to, shout and scream. Tear up the paper into tiny pieces and destroy it. How does that feel? Any better? Or do you want to do that once more?

Now, move on to your creative project and use some of this emotional energy to make some progress. Give it around 20 minutes. Then write down what you felt about this exercise. Did you feel a new kind of energy?

....
....
....
....
....
....
....
....
....
....
....
....
....
....
....
....
....
....

Colors and emotions

Colors are saturated with emotional impact: some colors feel soft and gentle, others more joyful and dynamic, or aggressive and violent, while others will invite a sense of introspection and meditation. With all this going on, it's clear that color can be a useful tool in expressing how we feel.

Now make list of emotions, such as anger, sadness, fear, disgust, impatience, wonder, joy, surprise, pleasure, tenderness, euphoria… Take a sheet of drawing paper and some paint. Choose an emotion to explore, taking some time to really concentrate on it. What range of colors will you use? Don't overthink it, just go with your intuition. Check on how you are feeling during this exercise. Do you still feel connected with the emotion you picked out at the start? When you are done, how about starting over, with another emotion?

HERE IS A SIMPLE SUMMARY OF COLORS AND THEIR SYMBOLISM

RED	POWER, PASSION, STRENGTH, COURAGE, ACTION, VITALITY
ORANGE	ENERGY, CREATIVITY, DYNAMISM
YELLOW	LIGHT, RADIANCE, SELF-CONFIDENCE, OPTIMISM, HAPPY-GO-LUCKY
GREEN	HOPE, NATURE, GROWTH, HARMONY, HEALING, ABUNDANCE
BLUE	PEACE, CONFIDENCE, CALM, EXPRESSION
INDIGO	FAITH, WISDOM, INTELLECT, GENEROSITY
VIOLET	MYSTERY, SPIRITUALITY, INTUITION, MEDITATION
WHITE	PURITY, INNOCENCE, SILENCE
BLACK	DEATH, GRIEF, NIGHT, DISTRESS, ELEGANCE

HOW DID THIS EXERCISE GO? WHAT EFFECT DID IT HAVE ON YOU? WHAT COLORS DID YOU CHOOSE?

....
....
....
....
....
....
....
....
....

IF YOU WISH TO KNOW MORE ABOUT THE FASCINATING SUBJECT OF COLOR, THEN HERE'S A USEFUL BOOK: *THE STORY OF COLOUR* BY GAVIN EVANS.

Creativity and emotions

Creativity is an incredible tool for expressing our emotions. Some creative people have a remarkable capacity to express and transmit emotion through their work. And this act of creating is liberating. In this exercise, pick up whatever drawing materials you want and create a picture, concentrating on your emotions and letting them drive the marks you make on the page, the form, the color, and any words too, if you like.

Then choose a specific emotion, such as anger or joy, and see how you could explore it in a drawing.

WHAT OTHER WAYS COULD YOU EXPRESS YOUR EMOTIONS?

Will it be through writing, drawing, collage, dance, sport, or maybe DIY? Take some to time to note down whatever ideas come to you, and then choose one technique to continue your emotional explorations.

....
....
....
....
....
....
....
....
....
....
....
....

Change how you're feeling

Whatever emotional state you're in right now, do yourself a favor and give your emotions a bit of space to express themselves. This simple exercise will allow you to gently connect with some positive emotions, and your emotional state will improve rapidly. First, make a list of all the pleasurable things that make you feel good. The more you put down, the better. It could be something very simple, like getting lost in a good book. Now cut out some rectangles from a sheet of printer paper. On each one, write down something from your list. Decorate them if you like. Then fold each one twice, and put them into a small bag: you are going to make a lucky pick! Select one at random, and then do what's shown on the paper—or take a step to making it happen. Not feeling better yet? Then pick out another one … until you start to feel your spirits lift.

HOW DO YOU FEEL NOW?

....
....
....
....
....
....

WHEN YOU'RE FEELING KIND OF LOW, PICK OUT ONE OF THESE LITTLE BITS OF PAPER!

Cultivating joy

DAY 281

The joy of joy

Joy is a feeling of intense pleasure, an opening up of our hearts, often linked to the achievement of our hopes and dreams. It is an emotion that can work its magic in all dimensions of our lives, affecting the brain's functioning by inhibiting cortisol, the stress hormone, and helping us instead feel relaxed in both body and mind. When we feel joy, everything seems easy. And if our creativity can give us joy, then joy too can help us reconnect with our creativity. It is a win-win scenario. Everything then falls into place. New ideas seem to come to us naturally, and the entire creative process becomes a pleasure in itself. We just don't want to stop.

WHAT PART DOES JOY PLAY IN YOUR LIFE?

What brings joy to your own heart, and what do you need to do to make that happen? What symbolizes joy for you? In today's exercise, use your imagination to come up with some thoughts that bring you joy. How could you put more joy into your life? Note down your ideas, however crazy they may seem. Is there one on your list that you could put into practice today?

....
....
....
....
....
....
....
....
....
....
....
....

A word about sadness

We all live through moments of sadness. Mostly, we get sad when we look back to the past with a sense of loss, either having lost something or someone, or sensing something missing from our lives. Deeper problems arise when we get stuck in a pattern of these sad reflections, which is where depression starts. Letting our unhappiness come to the surface can be a great personal strength, provided we can reflect on its meaning and move forward to a new phase of our lives. Oftentimes, this is easier said than done.

IS THERE SADNESS IN YOUR LIFE?

Does it come to you often, or not so often? Is your typical state somewhere between sadness and joy? How do you experience sadness? What messages can you draw from it? Have you figured out ways to cope, and what are they? Suppose you tried to put some distance between you and some of the people or things that make you feel down: people you feel are too negative, or subjects that you find boring or too serious. It's not about running away, but more about not letting yourself get dragged down.

WHAT ASPECTS OF YOUR LIFE COULD YOU CHANGE TO FEEL MORE OF A LIGHTNESS OF BEING?

....
....
....
....
....
....
....
....
....
....
....

The power of a smile

For today's exercise, stand in front of the mirror and smile. Not an empty smile, but one of your best and most heartfelt smiles, and keep it up, in the mirror, for several minutes, feeling the emotion mounting as you do so. This can be difficult to begin with, and you're going to feel like you're forcing it, but keep trying. After a while, you'll find the smile becoming more and more natural, and at the same time you will start to feel happier inside. Hold on to that feeling, and think about making your own creative journey more joyful, thanks to your smile.

Today, have a go at smiling at the people you come across, and see how they react. And observe also how you react, how you feel as a result. At the end of the day, write down how it went.

HOW DID IT GO TODAY?

....
....
....
....
....
....
....
....
....
....
....

Drawing out the joy

Take your notebook and draw some simple images of the sun, as a child would do. You can go on filling up pages of your notebook with these simple sun images, in whatever sizes, styles, and colors you want to use. Put a smiley face inside each sun, and go on adding whatever else to the pages—moons, stars, whatever: the idea is to make your drawings come alive with smiles, and then feel the joy. Now have fun coloring it all in. Do whatever feels good, and use this time to fill up with joy, gentleness, and love, basking in those smiles and kindness! When you're done, you could cut out the suns and put them around your home, sticking them to the fridge or a mirror, or hide them in drawers or even inside a pair of shoes. When you find one in a few weeks or months, it will bring a smile to your face.

Did you enjoy this exercise? Did you notice a change in your mood? Or did it make you feel ill at ease? Remember, be kind to yourself: do you want to continue, or maybe to draw something else?

HOW DO YOU FEEL NOW, COMPARED TO WHEN WHEN YOU STARTED THIS EXERCISE?

....
....
....
....
....
....
....
....
....

Let there be music

Music is a great way to change our mood almost instantly. What are your favorite songs? Start a list, and try to complete it over the coming days. Meanwhile, your task today is to put on some music that makes you feel joyful: sing your head off, and dance like there's nobody watching!

If you haven't already done so, make some playlists of your favorite joyful music: pieces that make you feel really good when you take the time to listen properly, and that make you want to dance. Write down what comes to mind for your playlist.

....
....
....
....
....
....
....
....
....
....
....
....
....

Laughter and humor

There is nothing like having a good laugh to put us into a joyful frame of mind, and in this exercise, take a moment to remember times when you were really laughing at something extremely funny. What memories come up for you? Could you write them down in some detail? Telling the story again, you have a chance to relive the moment once again, maybe evening smiling to yourself at the memory. Give yourself a chance to reconnect with your joyful spirit, and make a wish for more of these classic moments!

If nothing in particular comes to mind, don't worry about it. Think about films or TV series that make you laugh, or some moments spent with your family or friends, at school or on vacation: moments when you remember feeling really good.

....
....
....
....
....
....
....
....
....
....
....
....
....
....
....
....
....
....
....
....
....
....
....
....

Laugh for 10 minutes a day!

Creativity and a sense of humor are a powerful combo. According to an old saying, the path to staying healthy is to laugh for 10 minutes a day. Laughter is also a great ingredient for creativity. What makes you laugh? And what could you do to put more laughter into your life?

WHICH ARTISTS AND PERFORMERS MAKE YOU LAUGH AND SMILE?

Which films or TV series make you laugh, smile, or feel good? Which books or poems or comedy sketches have a similar effect? Maybe there are certain quotes that also put joy into your heart?

Make your own personal list, an antidote to feeling down, and today, put some time aside to laugh and smile. Then, go to work on your creative project. Do you see a difference in your creative mood? How could you use your creativity to put more humor into your life? Or, looking at it another way, how could you use your humor to put more creativity into your life?

....
....
....
....
....
....
....
....
....
....
....
....
....
....
....
....
....
....
....

Staying motivated

A lack of motivation

Knowing how to stay motivated is an essential part of our creative work. Of course, it is completely natural to feel our motivation drop from time to time. In fact, our motivation is a function of our inner state—our mood, thoughts, and emotions—and it's our job to try to decipher what these fluctuations actually mean.

How motivated are you in your various projects? Do you find it easy to stay motivated? Or do you get put off pretty easily? If so, why is that? What could you do to get more motivated?

That prime motivation that sparked your creative project may not be enough in itself to take the project through to completion. We are all human, circumstances change, and so do our priorities. That's life! Has this happened to you?

HOW DO YOU RESPOND WHEN YOU FEEL YOU HAVE LOST YOUR MOTIVATION, AND YOU'RE JUST NOT INTERESTED IN YOUR PROJECT ANYMORE?

....
....
....
....
....
....
....
....
....
....
....
....
....
....
....
....
....
....
....

DAY
289

Procrastination

It is possible to be very creative, to love our projects with a passion, but to still lack motivation, putting stuff off until later: the dreaded procrastination. It was thanks to the coach and motivational speaker David Laroche that I learned that motivation itself is not the culprit. If our projects inspire us and have real meaning for us, then our motivation will be right there where we need it. So if we find ourselves procrastinating, it's likely because either we have lost sight of the deeper meaning of what we are doing, or the meaning has evolved and no longer matches up with what we want. Once we spot that, getting motivation back becomes more within reach, and procrastination becomes less of a deal.

The first step is to redefine what really inspires you in your life and within your project, and get that creative fire burning again. What really motivates you in life? Can you describe that in a few words? What are your passions?

IF YOU FEEL A LACK OF MOTIVATION IN YOUR PROJECT, TRY TO LINK IT BACK TO THE THINGS THAT HAVE REAL MEANING FOR YOU IN YOUR LIFE. WHAT DOES YOUR PROJECT INSPIRE WITHIN YOU? WHAT MADE YOU WANT TO START IT?

....
....
....
....
....
....
....
....
....
....
....
....
....
....
....
....
....
....
....
....

Asking the question "Why?"

Today I'd like you to continue thinking about some of the questions that came up yesterday. Read back over your answers and then start a list of reasons why you feel strongly about your creative project, to the point where you start to feel a shift in your mood and a new enthusiasm.

HOW DO YOU FEEL HAVING JUST COMPLETED THIS LIST? CAN YOU SEE A DIFFERENCE? DOES IT MAKE YOU FEEL LIKE GOING BACK TO WORK ON YOUR PROJECT?

....
....
....
....
....
....
....
....
....
....
....
....
....
....
....
....
....
....

Take a few sheets of paper and rewrite your list several times, embellishing the pages as you wish. Then display the sheets in places where you will see them each day or maybe leave a copy in your creative happy box.

On a day when you feel your enthusiasm drop, read your lists out loud and with real meaning, until you start to feel a shift in your mood and motivation. Consider changing your list as time goes on, if you feel the need.

How to say "no"

By developing a strong and supportive mind-set, we can resist being drawn into negative and discouraging thoughts. Remember, you have a choice in all this: you can accept or resist a whole raft of thoughts, for better or for worse. If you can say no to lack of motivation, to discouragement, to your inner critic, and to those negative thoughts that seem to race away without you, then you really can recover your creative powers. "No" is an almost magical word that you can pronounce, with as much power as you can muster, to drive away these negative sentiments. So just say "No!" and "Stop!" and "I'm not going there!" And then you can say "Yes" to the things that you really do want. Think about those things for a moment, and then write them down, feeling your motivation and morale rising as you do so. Keep an eye on yourself today, and watch out for the thoughts and feelings that you accept, and those that you reject.

AT THE END OF YOUR DAY, WRITE DOWN YOUR OBSERVATIONS.

....
....
....
....
....
....
....
....
....
....
....
....
....
....
....
....
....
....
....
....

Changing the rhythm

Lack of motivation is sometimes a sign that we're tired. It could be physical tiredness, because we find it difficult to stop and rest, or a kind of emotional fatigue, linked with losing the meaning of our project, or, sometimes, our lives themselves. How good are you at listening to what your body needs in terms of rest and sleep? A good night's sleep can be the solution to many creative problems. But equally, lack of activity can also hit our creative energy, which is why physical activity can recharge your batteries. Going out for a walk for 20 minutes can be enough to get you thinking differently and leave you feeling energized.

WHAT DO YOU FIND USEFUL TO CHANGE YOUR RHYTHM? ARE YO[U] GOOD AT LISTENING TO WHAT YOUR BODY NEEDS? OR DO YOU SOMETIMES LEAVE IT TOO LATE?

A supportive team

The people around us can be influential on our moods. If you want to feel more motivated, you could try to surround yourself with some really get-up-and-go friends, and feed off of their energy.

Learn to seek encouragement from kind and trusted friends. Maybe you know some people already who you feel are on the same wavelength as you, and who could provide support and encouragement.

Another way is to get together with people in a similar creative path to your own. You will find that encouraging other people is a great way for us to find motivation ourselves. Is there anyone that you think you might link up with?

IF YOU HAVE OTHER CREATIVE PEOPLE TO SHARE YOUR EXPERIENCES WITH, CAN YOU MEET REGULARLY TO DISCUSS YOUR PROGRESS?

Your best moments

Do you remember times in your life when motivation was not a problem, and when everything seemed to fall into place? Perhaps you can recall moments when you felt creatively inspired, pushed along by invisible wings, full or dynamism and creative energy. Take a moment to think about these times, and write about them in your notebook. Detail how you felt, and those feelings may well return as you do so.

REREAD YOUR NOTES ABOUT AWESOME MOMENTS WHENEVER YOU NEED TO RECONNECT WITH YOUR MOTIVATION.

All about energy

DAY
295

When energy runs short

Learning how to make the best of our energy is vital to our creative process. We all experience drops in energy and mood and end up asking ourselves why we don't seem to have enough in the tank to get us to the end of our project. It happens to us all, because when we are tired we can quickly believe that nothing is going right. The good news is there are plenty of easy ways out of this. The trick is to make the decision to do something about it, and right away! We have to stop believing that we are the victims of malevolent forces and external conditions, and instead get back into the driver's seat of our lives. Simply making that mental step can give us an amazing level of energy, believing that from now on, we are the ones in charge, ready to resume the creative life that we desire. So let's get started!

> "THE KEY TO A **PASSIONATE** LIFE IS TO TRUST AND FOLLOW THE ENERGY WITHIN US."
>
> —SHAKTI GAWAIN

TODAY, MONITOR YOUR ENERGY LEVELS

Watch for any changes in your level of energy as you go through your day. How do you manage your energy? Do you ever feel like you have too much, or too little? How do you expend your energy? And how do you boost it? What could you do today to improve your energy levels?

....

....

....

....

....

....

....

....

....

....

Wasted energy

Sometimes we spend pretty much all of our precious energy focusing on what's going wrong, stuff that we hate, and things we don't have. Without realizing, we can run out of gas for the things that really matter in our lives, including our creative projects. By wanting things to match up exactly with some kind of blueprint of our own making, we can get ridiculously obsessed with complaining when everything doesn't go to plan.

It's time to free yourself from this way of thinking. Start by looking at how you might be blocking or wasting energy. Do you spend time complaining and moaning? Are you more of a pessimist than an optimist? And too much eating, sleeping, or simply sitting around will also lead to a sense of lost energy.

ARE YOU AWARE OF WHAT DRAGS YOU DOWN? MAKE A LIST, WITH EXAMPLES. WHAT COULD YOU ELIMINATE FROM THE LIST TO LEAVE YOU WITH MORE ENERGY?

....
....
....
....
....
....
....
....
....
....
....
....
....

Using what you've got

Sometimes we find ourselves on a frenetic creative high. Other times, it's the opposite, and we feel slow and peaceful. High—or low—levels of creative energy are useful at different stages of the creative cycle, and your awareness of your energy state will allow you to make a conscious choice of the kind of activity that is the right fit for you on any given day. Creativity does not always need you to put the pedal to the metal, and the early ideas stage needs more concentration than, say, the fabrication stage. Can you read your own creative energy during your projects? If not, monitor your progress over the coming days and weeks and see what you discover.

YOU CAN DO THIS EXERCISE USING WRITING, PHOTOGRAPHY, MUSIC, OR DANCE—WHATEVER YOU PREFER.

WHY NOT TEST OUT DIFFERENT KINDS OF ENERGY WITH SOME DRAWING OR PAINTING?

Wait for a time when you sense a powerful wave of creative energy within yourself, and see how it can be expressed through drawing or painting. Do the same exercise when the energy seems to be gentler, slower, and deeper.

WRITE DOWN WHAT YOU OBSERVED.

....
....
....
....
....
....
....
....
....

A different quality of energy

Today, I'd like you to try an exercise that will help lift your mood, boost your energy, and get you set to work on your creative projects. By calling to mind what's really close to our hearts, we get in a better mood to be creative. As long as this process makes you feel good, you should use it as often as you like.

For around 10 to 15 minutes, write down the things you love the most in your life—whatever comes to mind. They could be people, places, simple things, or amazing things. Then, continue the list, this time with the things you love about your creative projects, and the project you are working on right now. Next, describe *why* you love these things. For example, you love to create as a way of thanking those who believe in you, or to inspire others, or for the beauty of art, or for your own personal pleasure.

*I love*_____ *because*_____

....
....
....
....
....
....
....
....

TO FINISH OFF, READ THE LIST OUT LOUD. NOTE HOW YOU FELT AT THE START OF THE EXERCISE, AND AT THE END. DO YOU SEE A DIFFERENCE?

....
....
....
....
....
....
....
....
....

Your best creative moments

When we are feeling weak and worn out, a particularly effective pick-me-up is to reconnect with those intense levels of energy that we experienced during some of our most creative moments. By looking back and remembering these awesome creative moments, we have a chance to examine our own creative dynamic and how that felt at the time. It can also help us recreate that mind-set when we need it the most.

CLOSE YOUR EYES AND TRY TO REMEMBER ...

When in your life have you felt really inspired and really creative? Perhaps there was a time when you scored a significant creative win, a major breakthrough, when you felt on a creative high, as if anything were possible. Go back through your memories and note down anything that comes to mind. Try to reconnect with the feelings you experienced at the time, to see if you can relive them, calling on them for support when you need to. Try to reexperience those moments for all they're worth. Do you manage to feel the same kind of joy and enthusiasm?

....
....
....
....
....
....
....
....
....
....
....
....
....
....
....
....
....
....
....

What gives you energy?

Think about what in your life gives you energy. Make a list of at least 20 ideas. Everything that gets us moving creates some kind of inner change, and causes our energy levels to rise. The main thing is to keep on seeking more and higher levels of energy. It works like a muscle: the more we train ourselves to boost our energy, the better we become at it.

It could be active things like physical exercise. Or more gentle activities like taking a nap, or more "mental" exercises like doing a Sudoku, or spiritual things like meditation.

Using the table below, make your own list of energy-giving activities, which you can go on adding to as you discover new things.

PHYSICAL	GENTLE	MENTAL AND SPIRITUAL

DEPENDING ON THE ENERGY LEVEL YOU HAVE NOW AND WHAT YOU WANT TO ACHIEVE, CHOOSE AN ACTIVITY FROM YOUR LIST AND DO IT RIGHT NOW!

Creative visualization

Take a moment to focus on your breathing. Then, sit comfortably, placing your feet flat on the ground. Close your eyes and imagine that your feet are putting down roots into the ground, which run deep below the earth until they reach an immense subterranean reservoir, the size of a continent, which is full of nourishment for your creativity. Feel the pleasure of your roots drawing up those creative resources, filling you with energy, right through to every last cell in your body: full of joy, sparkle, energy, passion, creativity, enthusiasm, and love.

Now start to move, stand up, jump, move your limbs in every direction, and if you like, put on some music and dance until you feel completely revitalized.

WHAT WAS THIS EXPERIENCE LIKE? HOW DO YOU FEEL NOW?

....
....
....
....
....
....
....
....
....
....
....
....
....
....
....
....
....
....

Confidence

DAY 302

Self-confidence

Having confidence in ourselves means being able to make things happen. Self-confidence is not an innate quality. Rather, it is something that is developed and strengthened throughout our lives, and it has a major effect on how successful we can be, creatively. Each of us has our own style of self-confidence, and we nurture it over our lives in our own way according to our unique mix of personality, history, experiences, and so on.

What gives you confidence? How do you develop self-confidence in the creative fields? If you had more confidence in yourself, what would you like to create? Which projects would you embark on? What creative opportunities would you want to take up?

WRITE DOWN WHAT COMES TO MIND

Imagine how you might be in six months' time, feeling more self-confident: what would your creative life be like? What would you have accomplished? What could you put in place today to go in this direction?

....
....
....
....
....
....
....
....

Recognizing your own value

There is nothing better for building self-confidence than taking a closer look at what we are good at. By recognizing our own value, we can boost our level of confidence in ourselves. We can develop a quiet certainty that we have what it takes to be creative, and to follow our projects through to completion. By each incremental advance in a project, we can prove to ourselves that we have the capacity to continue. Sometimes, we can be reluctant to push ourselves forward, afraid we may shine too brightly. But hey: valuing our own skills takes nothing away from anybody else!

DO YOU TEND TO PLAY DOWN YOUR OWN VALUE?

Reflect a little on whether you tend not to recognize your own value, and if this acts as a brake on how you bring your talents forward to the world. Start by making a list of your qualities, skills, and knowledge. By putting this in writing, you are giving yourself permission to acknowledge all of these qualities, and you'll become more aware of your own potential.

WHAT ARE YOUR QUALITIES AND SKILLS? WHERE DO YOUR TALENTS LIE?

What have been your big creative successes: those which you personally are extremely proud of? What did you have to overcome to make them happen, and how did this affect your self-confidence? Did you discover new resources within yourself, making you feel more complete and more balanced as a result? What have you been working on creatively since starting this book? Can you transform setbacks and difficulties so that you can learn from them and grow?

IF YOU FEEL THE NEED, **REREAD WEEK 7, "YOU'RE WORTH IT!"** TO GET A SENSE OF YOUR PROGRESS.

The power of repetition

Regular training leads to improvement. And by getting better at something, we are almost certain to boost self-confidence. The really powerful improvements come from repetition, learning one step at a time, and almost all expertise comes about from intensive practice, repeating the same actions until they are totally mastered. It's an automatic mechanism, and we can all do it. The more time you spend, the better you get. So if, for example, you want to feel confident at drawing, then simply draw, draw, and draw some more!

In which creative areas would you like to boost your confidence? And what creative techniques would you like to be able to improve on? How could you reorganize your life to give you time to boost these skills? Set aside some slots in your day to give you time to practice, and then, in a month's time, check out the progress you have made.

....
....
....
....
....
....
....
....
....
....
....
....
....
....
....
....
....
....
....
....
....

Confidence in the process

In the middle of the creative process there can often be moments of doubt when nothing seems to go right; times when we have to dig deep within ourselves to find a few ounces of self-confidence to take us through. These are tough times, and it can be hard to see them as opportunities to learn and reflect, as if all these obstacle in our path have some kind of meaning. Getting through this means keeping the faith with the creative process, which in turn means letting the process run its course, even if we can feel rather powerless at times.

DO YOU HAVE CONFIDENCE IN THE CREATIVE PROCESS?

Do you manage to remain confident in the process even when everything looks chaotic? If so, how? What could you put in place to keep your project on track?

If you feel the need, reread Day 239 ("Staying on course"). Write down what inspires you to feel more confident, and check back on what you wrote down at that time. Does it still feel right, or do you feel you'd like to make a new list of "Why?" questions. Compare the two lists. Are there differences? If there are, what do you think has changed?

....
....
....
....
....
....
....
....
....
....
....
....
....
....
....
....

Dare to do more

By pushing ourselves to new limits, we find a new pride in our abilities and alter how we see ourselves. This can seriously reinforce our image of ourselves, becoming someone who can go further, be more creative, and react faster—leading to us gaining more self-confidence with each step we take. We can start to believe that we do indeed have the creative resources we need, and even if we hit a bump in the road, we have the skills to turn it into an opportunity. The goal is not so much success, but the pride of having accomplished our project. Just by getting to the end we can be proud of what we have done, and our perception of ourselves can be transformed.

WHAT STEPS CAN YOU TAKE IN YOUR CREATIVE PROJECT TODAY?

What could you do today to push that little bit harder and further in your own creative project? Will you be proud of yourself once it is complete? If not, maybe you could find a bigger step to take, bringing your project to a whole new level. Or, more simply, you could make some adjustments to ensure that your project is more closely matched with your hopes and aspirations, so that you can feel more satisfied when you get to the conclusion.

....
....
....
....
....
....
....
....
....
....
....
....
....
....
....

Setting challenges

Giving ourselves challenges is like doing a self-confidence workout. By exercising our own self-belief, and pushing that little bit further, we can make big gains in self-confidence. So let's challenge ourselves to go beyond our fears and doubts, and leave our old habits and need for reassurance behind.

What kind of fears and doubts are there in your life (creative, or more generally) at the moment? Conquering these fears and setting new challenges is a sure way to boost our self-confidence in all walks of life, which in turn will help in creative pursuits too. Pick one of your fears or doubts, and think of three different ways you could transform it into a challenge. Choose one of these, and tackle it today. Then, write about your experience. How did it go? Did you surprise yourself? Did you learn from the experience? And importantly, congratulations for having a go!

A MANTRA TO BOOST SELF-CONFIDENCE

Find a quote that inspires you and gives you confidence. Adapt it if necessary so that it really resonates with you. Repeat it, without stopping, to give you the courage to push yourself even further, growing in confidence.

....
....
....
....
....
....
....
....
....
....
....
....
....
....
....

Something bigger

Whatever our religious beliefs may or may not be, believing in a positive force that underpins our lives can be a further source of confidence for many people. If we can believe that life itself is on our side, going along with us in our direction, and that we are loved, then this certainty can give us strength and make us more creative. Believing in something bigger than ourselves is to believe that, even if we can't make sense of our lives right now, a meaning does exist and it will become clear when we need it to. If we believe in a kind of superior wisdom, then we don't have to give up on our own free will, but we can decide that the lives that we lead are the best for ourselves. And even if we can't really figure out how, things will eventually fall into place, both in our lives and in our creative projects. In short, we don't need to be in control of everything.

DO YOU TRUST IN A HIGHER POWER?

Do you believe in something bigger than all of us? Do you feel that the forces of life are on your side? How could you develop even more faith in life? What steps could you put into place today to achieve this?

Draw a symbol of your own faith in life. What would it look like? A star, perhaps, or an angel, or some form of presence? Take some colored pencils and in the box below, express whatever comes to mind.

Authenticity

Being authentic

DAY 309

To be authentic is to be true to ourselves and to others. It is the link with our true nature, which exists quite apart from all the trappings of social conditioning and conventions, from culture and from education.

Rules, of course, are essential to allow us to learn to live in a community with one another. But the price we pay for this is to cut off some of our deepest instincts. Of course, we absolutely need to be able to live socially with each other, but there is a "domestication," if you will, of our more animal instincts, which leads to a kind of fog lying between who we are, what we show of ourselves to the world, and what we manage to create. And this can lead to a lot of pain. To rediscover something of our authentic selves is going to require some honesty and courage to look at ourselves frankly and see aspects of ourselves that we don't like. It's time to step out of the easy comfort of our everyday lives!

AUTHENTICITY FORCES US TO ASK AN ESSENTIAL QUESTION: WHO ARE WE, REALLY?
It is not an easy question to answer. It takes perseverance to find answers, but our creativity will come out of this process stronger and more dynamic.

> ❝ BE YOURSELF, EVERYONE ELSE IS ALREADY TAKEN. ❞
> —OSCAR WILDE

Do you feel totally true to yourself? And with those around you? These questions can be unsettling, making us feel ill at ease, and so be kind to yourself as you reflect on them. Do you reveal your true self and your creativity without fear? Do you see differences in when you can be your natural self and when you feel less free? If you could be more authentic, what would you do? Who would you be?

WRITE DOWN WHAT COMES TO MIND, AS WELL AS YOUR FEELINGS AND ANY OTHER QUESTIONS RAISED BY THESE REFLECTIONS. ADD TO THESE NOTES OVER THE FOLLOWING DAYS.

Role-play

All of us grow up with a childhood built around disguises imposed by those around us, by our families and by wider society. We figure out that to be loved and accepted, we have to behave in a certain way and meet the expectations of those around us. But wearing these kinds of masks can end up obscuring—even to us—who we really are.

Reflect for a moment on the roles that you played in the past, and that perhaps you continue to play, but that are not really you. Perhaps they're cutting you off from part of who you are. Be patient and kind with yourself as you think back on these things.

Which kinds of characters do you recognize in yourself? Are you trying to be perfect? Are you ultra-polite? Maybe you pretend to be very calm? Are you the comedian? Or the snarky one? Suppose you were to drop these characters and simply be you: what would happen?

Take a moment to figure out what kind of personalities—or masks—you find yourself wearing most of the time. Make a list, perhaps giving each one an amusing name. You could even have a go at drawing them as caricatures. Have fun, and be kind to yourself: these characters express certain aspects—certain needs, perhaps—but do not define your deepest nature.

How are you feeling now? A little unsettled, maybe, or perhaps more aware of yourself? Ready to be a little kinder to yourself? Or a bit fragile?

WRITE DOWN YOUR IMPRESSIONS.

....
....
....
....
....
....
....
....
....
....
....
....
....
....
....
....
....

Using creativity

For the following exercise, you will need to find a place where you won't be disturbed. Settle yourself someplace comfortable, close your eyes, and take a deep breath. Call to mind your inner child. Feel their presence right alongside you. Now take your paints and a large sheet of drawing paper, and start by painting a mask that represents all the roles that you have played in the past. Have as much fun with this as possible, working up that creative energy. When you're done, cut out the mask, turn it over, and on the other side paint a representation of your own true face.

HOW DID IT GO? AND HOW ARE YOU FEELING NOW?

....
....
....
....
....
....
....
....
....
....
....

Authenticity and creativity

The more authentic we can be, the more our creativity will be sincere. The results don't matter. If we are only creating to please an audience, then this will be all too evident in our work: it may lack soul, meaning we will end up deeply dissatisfied. If we can create with all our authenticity, then we are learning to be ourselves, and to show who we are to the world, without pretense. So we need to accept our imperfections, our errors, and just be ourselves. If we can create with authenticity, then we must also answer the question: why are we doing this? And it is not always easy to answer.

Why do you create? To be seen and recognized? Or from a desire to succeed? Or to meet the needs of other people? Do you crave admiration? Or, on the other hand, perhaps you are creating in harmony with your deepest sense of self, because it feels right? Do you fully embrace what you create? Do you accept your mistakes and imperfections?

How could you be more authentic in your creativity, and be even more in tune with your inner self? Are your creative projects really your own? Or are they responding to the demands of those around you?

NOTE YOUR RESPONSES OVER THE HOURS AND DAYS THAT FOLLOW.

....
....
....
....
....
....
....
....
....

WHICH ARTISTS DO YOU THINK ARE THE MOST AUTHENTIC? AND WHY? HOW DO THEY INSPIRE YOU TO BECOME MORE AUTHENTIC?

....
....
....
....
....
....
....
....

Getting back to yourself

Cultivating authenticity is a practice that never ends, and it is almost inevitable that we lose track of it from time to time. Each time it is lost and found, we learn something new about ourselves. Even if we feel that we have lost our way, our deepest selves and instincts will never leave us, and it does not take much to reconnect with these. Discovering and rediscovering our authenticity is a route that demands the courage to swim against the tide of society and those around us. We have to dismantle the "false self" that no longer corresponds with who we really are, and when we do that, we find that we can only be satisfied through the pursuit of our true selves, so that we are peace with ourselves and in harmony with life.

As you move closer to your true self, here is another question: what is important for you?

WHAT MAKES YOUR HEART SING?
How could you encourage yourself to cultivate your authenticity? Live more in the present moment? Try out some meditation or contemplation? How about listening to those inner conversations? What are they telling you? Take some time to let your responses come to the surface over the coming hours and days.

....
....
....
....
....
....
....
....
....
....
....
....
....
....
....
....

Simplicity

To rediscover the route back to authenticity, one vital aid is simplicity. If we want to come back to the heart of things, we need to try to keep our minds out of the picture. Our minds love complicating things, and that is something that we can do without. A sense of simplicity invites us to come back to the projects that nourish our inner spirit, that are truly close to our hearts. It's an easy choice. Gone are the projects that were based on a bunch of illusory or complex ideas and that will never see the light of day.

What could you simplify in your life to live with more authenticity? Reduce your hours? Sort stuff out more often? Limit yourself to just two projects at any one time? What could you do to put you more in touch with simplicity?

NOTE DOWN YOUR IDEAS, AND PUT INTO PRACTICE THOSE THAT INSPIRE YOU THE MOST.

....
....
....
....
....
....
....
....
....
....

How about asking your heart to inspire you to help simplify your life and your creations?

Lie down and place your hands over your heart, until you can feel it beating. Breathe deeply. Use all your senses, and feel the presence of your body in the space you occupy. Imagine you are diving deeply down into your very self, to the heart of your heart … and you find that you are there, within, and always have been. There is nothing to prove, you are already there. You are … you!

Dare to show your vulnerability

When we are in the middle of a creative project, it can feel risky to share our research with others, and especially our difficulties or problems, as it can leave us feeling fragile and exposed: the project is not finished, and we have nothing, yet, to show for it. But if we can get over this, we can create a moment of sharing that can take us further than we could ever imagine. Accepting our vulnerability means accepting that we are not perfect. Sharing our vulnerabilities gives others the chance to see us as we really are, and gives us the amazing opportunity to be loved for who we really are too.

There is always that nagging question in the background: if I lift my mask, will they still love me? Some may not. But as the life coach and speaker David Laroche puts it: "I would rather be loved and hated for who I am, than loved for who I am not!"

How do you deal with your own vulnerability? Do you dare to show it to others? Do you feel vulnerable? Is this a problem for you? What would it feel like to share your creative process with someone you trusted? Do you remember times when you dared to show your vulnerability, and where it led to an unexpected sharing of experiences?

NOTE DOWN YOUR THOUGHTS AND FEELINGS.

....
....
....
....
....
....
....
....
....
....
....
....
....
....
....
....
....
....
....

Relations with others

> IF YOU WANT TO GO FAST, GO ALONE. IF YOU WANT TO GO FAR, GO TOGETHER.
>
> —AFRICAN PROVERB

DAY 316

The people around you

Sometimes, we can feel isolated in our creativity. So being able to gather a like-minded group of supportive and stimulating friends can be a huge benefit. Of course, not everyone around us will be equally into our creative endeavors, and as time goes on, we learn who to turn to for that vital support. The main thing is to accept the others for who they are, with kindness, love, and respect, but without expecting them to be something they are not.

Who do you have around you, and how helpful are they in your creative journey? Who in particular are you able to talk to about your own creative work? What could you change in those around you to find more inspiration and support for your creativity? What kind of people would you like to have around you? How could you meet such people?

TAKE TIME TODAY TO LOOK AT THOSE AROUND YOU, AND WRITE DOWN ANY THOUGHTS THAT COME IN RESPONSE TO THESE QUESTIONS.

....
....
....
....
....
....
....
....
....
....
....
....

How others see us

Wanting recognition from others is a natural part of who we all are. Problems can arise when our sense of our own value comes almost exclusively from how others see us. At that point, it can distort everything: we become addicted to it, and our own sense of self gets trampled. In creative terms, the problem is linked with our efforts to please everyone with our work, at which point we begin to turn away from our own authenticity. We start second-guessing our audience, trying to figure out what they want to see from us. In reality, this displays a huge hole in our self-esteem. And we can end up judging ourselves in terms of what we get back from everyone else.

How do you deal with how others see your creative work? Do you feel you rely on this to feel valued? Do you feel addicted to the views of an audience? How so? Are you afraid of showing your work, and afraid of criticism? If so, what do you really expect from the outside world viewing your work? Are you afraid of being found out, found wanting? How can you use your creativity to get around this fixation with others' opinions, and boost your confidence in your own abilities? What would be the first step?

....
....
....
....
....
....
....
....
....
....
....
....
....
....
....
....

Time to revisit

Take some time to think about the preceding questions and see what responses you have. You may want to reread Week 7, where we talk about value, as well as Week 44 on self-confidence, particularly Day 302 and Day 303. Take another look also at Week 24 on critics and judgment. Choose whichever exercises resonate most with you, aiming to shore up your self-esteem and boost your confidence.

GO BACK OVER YOUR RESPONSES IN THOSE SECTIONS, AND NOTE DOWN ANY NEW THOUGHTS AND FEELINGS.

....
....
....
....
....
....
....
....
....
....
....
....
....
....

Comparisons, jealousy, and rivalry

A sense of competition is woven into the fabric of our society. To feel that we really belong, it is easy to believe that we need to be the smartest, the most creative, the most admired, the best of the best! The problem is that we can quickly get down on ourselves because we are not at the top of the tree, and this can lead to envy, rivalry, and jealousy. It is completely normal to feel challenged by the creative work of others. But if we start comparing a work that is finished and highly successful (by our judgment) with our own unfinished embryo of an idea, then we are not giving ourselves much of a chance here. At the same time, by feeling envy toward others, we can quickly forget that our own skills and attributes remain strong and undiminished. Instead, we act like their success has stolen something from us and left us lacking.

Where do you stand on all this? Do you compare yourself with others? How do you feel the challenge of other peoples' creative work: does it spur you to get back to work on your own project? Or do you start dreaming about their success?

Take some time to focus on your talents, skills, and qualities, your competences and accomplishments, and on the feeling of your own personal value. Make a list of the qualities you envy in others who are working in your own chosen discipline. Do you feel challenged by these? How can you respond to this challenge, to develop personally?

....
....
....
....
....
....
....
....
....
....
....
....
....
....
....
....
....
....
....
....

Creativity and relationships

We don't often think about how much creativity there is in our relationships—even if it can often be an almost magical ingredient adding exciting new flavors! Where are you in terms of creativity in your own relationships? How about doing a bit of a study of all the relationships you have with those close to you. How much of it all is routine? What kind of relationships would you really like to create? How could you do things differently with those around you, and with whom in particular? Would you like to change something? How could you be more creative in your love life? Could you create more closeness, complicity, playfulness, and joy in these relationships?

Take some time to write down your thoughts on each relationship, keeping it simple, and without judging. Then, imagine how you could put more creativity into each of these relationships, breaking out of the usual routines. For example, you could do a blind tasting of some new dishes together, organize a fancy dress dinner, go out in a new part of town, spend the night camping out or rent a cabin in the woods, go to a music festival, or simply give a friend a surprise present… How can you get started?

....
....
....
....
....
....
....
....
....
....
....
....
....
....
....

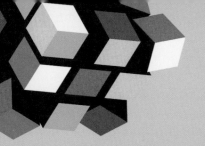

Appreciating the creativity in other people

Our own creativity will grow through contact with that of other people. By recognizing that people around us can also be inspiring, we can raise the bar for our own creativity and continue to learn and improve. Putting ourselves in contact with other creative people is exciting, and can leave us feeling enthused, celebrating their creativity, their own personal qualities, and their successes, spurring us on to go out and create for ourselves.

Who do you find inspiring? Do you recognize their creative qualities? In which field? Have you noticed how appreciating other people's creativity can stimulate you to accomplish your own projects? Which artists or mentors (alive or dead) are important to you, and why? What special qualities do you see in them? If you feel a close connection with them, how can you deepen this sense? Could you discover more about their own creative process? Or even get in touch with them or those who know or knew them? Which biographies would you read?

NOTE DOWN YOUR THOUGHTS AND ANY IDEAS THAT INSPIRE YOU.

Getting creative help

Knowing how to ask for help from other people is a way of multiplying our own creative powers. It shows that we have enough confidence in ourselves—and in them—to be able to share openly with them, without fear. By daring to tell them we need help, we are inviting the other person to express their own creativity, which is a beautiful gift to them, and to us. We expose our own vulnerability, our limits, and we offer the other person a chance to share the very best of themselves and, in the process, open up unseen avenues towards new creative thinking.

Have you received help on one of your projects at a time when you most needed it? How did that happen? Are you feeling blocked now, at a certain stage in your creative process? What sort of help could you ask for? And from whom? Do you have close friends who are also engaged in creative activities with whom you could share your experiences? How about getting in touch with them today. And if nobody comes to mind, you could ask the help of the universe, and of life itself: perhaps you will cross paths with someone new.

NOTE DOWN ANY THOUGHTS AND FEELINGS THAT COME AS A RESPONSE TO THESE QUESTIONS.

A creative team

Creativity is contagious. It can be incredibly stimulating to create alongside other people, releasing boundless energy and fusing together disparate ideas. Certain friendships between famous painters (such as Gaugin and Van Gogh) played a large part in the development of their respective talents. Working together from time to time, they inspired and influenced each other, and their friendship and mutual respect saw them flourish, each on their own distinct path.

Suppose you were to organize some collective workshop sessions with a group of creative people. You would each be talking about your own creative lives and projects, finding stimulation, nourishment, and a new creative spark. If your creative worlds are vastly different, then so much the better! Do you think you could organize weekly or monthly meetings? Are you tempted to start up a communal creative project? Or how about starting up a creative workshop with close friends, or even your kids? Who could join you? Are you tempted? Note down some ideas, send out some invitations, and make the date in your diary!

WHEN YOU'VE MADE IT HAPPEN, WRITE ABOUT IT HERE.

Love

DAY 324

Self-love

Love itself begins with our own love for ourselves, our bodies, our lives, and our unique presence in this world. Loving ourselves means appreciating our own value, and being able to support ourselves unconditionally during tough times, just as we would expect a loving parent to do. It's about accepting us as we are: our weaknesses and strengths, our fears as well as our courage. And it is also about giving ourselves what's needed to live as we wish, to have a life that is rich in experiences, creative, and contented. Loving ourselves means leaving aside judgment, criticism, harshness, demands for perfection—both in our daily lives, and of course, in all of our creative activities too.

Where do you stand in terms of your own self-love? What aspects of yourself do you love? Are there aspects you don't like? Suppose you were to try to encourage yourself to love yourself more than you do—much more, unconditionally? What would that change in your life, and in your creative life too?

TAKE SOME TIME TO ANSWER THESE QUESTIONS, AND NOTE DOWN YOUR ANSWERS OVER THE COMING DAYS.

....
....
....
....
....
....
....
....
....
....

Now find a comfortable and quiet place to sit. Close your eyes and place your hand gently over your heart and feel it beating, present in your life exclusively for you. Make a vow that from today on, your heart will be your guide to help you cultivate a deep love for yourself. Ask yourself how it might help guide you in your creativity—perhaps by allowing you to express more love within your creative work. **Allow time to return to yourself, and note down any thoughts and feelings.**

....
....
....
....
....
....
....
....

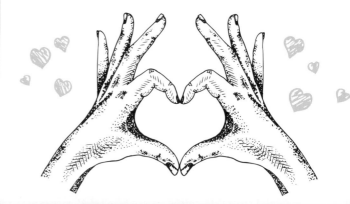

Say it out loud

By taking the step of loving ourselves, we are preparing some fertile ground for creativity. Author Louise Hay has written much about self-love, and believes that to love and accept ourselves exactly as we are will allow us to express the very best of ourselves, too. Now I would like you to have a go at one of Louise Hay's exercises.

Close your eyes and focus solely on your heart for a few minutes. Go up to a mirror and look yourself in the eyes, and say out loud to yourself: "I, (name), I love you." Continue by detailing the aspects of yourself in particular that you love for a further 10 minutes and say them out loud. Take time to savor the moment and the feelings it evokes.

WRITE DOWN YOUR FIRST IMPRESSIONS. HOW DID IT GO?

....
....
....
....
....
....
....
....
....
....
....

Feeling the love

Taking time to reflect on what we really love in our lives is a great way stay in a positive frame of mind, and this can bring about a marked change in our energy, leading us to feel a lightness of being, more joyful, and in a better place to get back to our creative projects. Write down what you love, noting down everything that comes to mind, and then say why, to the point where you can actually feel the love.

Here are a few ideas: What qualities in yourself do you love? What do you love about your body? Or in your life, or in your creative life? Who are the people who represent the very best of love, tenderness, and compassion? Maybe they are religious or spiritual leaders, or simply our beautiful planet. Find pictures of them and put them up in your house. If they could speak, what would they say to you?

NOTE DOWN YOUR RESPONSES, AND ANY NEW IDEAS THAT COME TO MIND DURING THE NEXT FEW HOURS. AT THE END OF THE EXERCISE, NOTE DOWN HOW YOU FEEL. HAS YOUR ENERGY CHANGED, AND IF SO, HOW?

....
....
....
....
....
....
....
....
....
....
....
....
....

Loving the roadblocks

Our first reaction when meeting an obstacle on our creative path is to want to get rid of it. But there is another way, which involves looking at these difficulties in a completely new light: with the greatest love that we can muster. The benefits of this are amazing: we can let go of the fear and anxiety, blockages seem to melt away, and so does the drama, irritation, and discouragement. We end up calmer, allowing our inner resources to come back into play. Our vision becomes clearer of what we are trying to express, and we can find the ideas and actions needed to get our projects back on track. In effect, we are going with the natural flow of our creative energy by learning to love our difficulties, imperfections, and errors. It's not easy, but by loving ourselves every step of the way, and giving our love to whatever befalls us on our journey, we will grow in our own self-love. It will take practice, of course. But try it out, and see what happens.

Do you manage to love the difficulties you face on your creative path? Have you already noticed how an obstacle can be transformed into a valuable gift by the power of love? Do you have examples of this happening in your own life?

WRITE DOWN YOUR EXPERIENCES IN YOUR NOTEBOOK.

....
....
....
....
....
....
....
....
....
....
....
....
....
....
....

Are you having to deal with a particular difficulty at the moment? Thinking carefully about this problem, take some time to listen to the beating of your heart. Feel the love that is within you spread out like a glorious light across your body, embracing the difficulty that you have been experiencing. Bask in this sensation to the point where you feel a change within you. Then come back to yourself and write about your experience. Did you feel something shift?

NOTE DOWN ANYTHING THAT CHANGES OVER THE DAYS THAT FOLLOW.

....
....
....
....
....
....
....
....
....
....

Problem softener

Now it's time to create a recipe that will use the power of love in a transformative way. The idea here is to change some old habits. Make a list of things that you do not like, and transform how you think about them using the power of love!

Now you can make your very own "problem softener." What is the key ingredient? Love! Are you going through a particular creative difficulty at the moment? Or perhaps in your life? Take a sheet of paper and draw the outline of a big container of fabric softener. Fill up your container with text, writing the words that inspire you: love, kindness, compassion, energy, creative, softness… Then, cut out the finished container.

Think about the specific difficulty you are facing, and address it out loud: "Yes, you, my difficulty, I accept you and I recognize you. Look, I have made a special recipe just for you." Imagine you can pour your concoction onto the difficulty, surrounding it in the power of love.

HOW DID YOU FIND THIS EXERCISE? DID YOU SENSE A SHIFT IN ENERGY? WAS IT HELPFUL? DO YOU HAVE NEW IDEAS?

....
....
....
....
....
....
....
....
....
....
....
....
....

Create with your heart

DAY 329

>
> THE PROJECT IS JUST A PRETEXT: WE PRACTICE OUR ART TO BE IN TUNE WITH OUR HEARTS, SO THAT OUR LIVES REFLECT THIS CONNECTION.
> —ANNE-MARIE JOBIN

I believe that art needs to be guided by love. Of course, there are plenty of creative people out there who turn their personal pain into magnificent works of art, and I am sure they too have a deep love of art. But I feel that by connecting to the source of life, or to something that's bigger than all of us, we can bring peace, joy, happiness, and love into our work. By making this connection with our heart, and by loving what we create, and through creating what we love, we are letting creativity express itself through us. But it all depends on what you want to create, and why you want to do this.

WHAT PLACE DOES LOVE TAKE IN YOUR OWN CREATIVITY TODAY?

Do you love to create? What is it about creating that you love? And why? Do you love the creative process? How could you love it even more? Do you love your creations too?

....
....
....
....
....
....
....
....
....
....
....

Before you start work on your creative project, take 5 minutes to focus on your heart. Feel the love growing within you and filling your whole body, and then set to work with your project, staying as closely connected as you can with your heart and with love.

HOW DID IT GO? DID ANYTHING FEEL DIFFERENT? DID SOMETHING FEEL SPECIAL?

....
....
....
....
....
....
....
....
....
....
....
....
....
....

Love, relationships, and creativity

Our creativity is an amazing tool to demonstrate our love of life and of those around us. The possibilities are endless! Close your eyes and take a deep breath. Visualize your inner child, and get them to help you develop love and creativity in all of your relations with other people.

WHAT NEW IDEAS DID YOU PICK UP?

How could you show more love to those around you? How could you express your love in your daily life, using aspects of your creativity?

....
....
....
....
....
....
....
....

Now, write down words of love and encouragement on some small scraps of paper. Fold them and hide them around your home. Basically, just have fun leaving them anyplace you like. Then forget about them, and watch people smile when they turn one up in a few weeks or months! Could you imagine how you might show a bit more of your love to those close to you? Maybe write them love letters and send them in the mail?

NOTE DOWN THE IDEAS THAT COME TO MIND, THEN DO ONE OF THEM.

....
....
....
....
....
....
....
....
....

Gratitude

DAY 331

The benefits of gratitude

The act of saying thank you can be a powerful one. It is a moment when we open our hearts with a sense of joy to what the world has given us. We are no longer just waiting for something else, because everything that exists in our lives becomes a precious gift that meets every one of our needs. So no more frustrations, as we learn to value even the smallest things in our lives and we glow with pleasure at being alive and being able to create. Everything becomes easier, and we can feel an incredible sense of freedom by realizing that what we have is sufficient. Feeling gratitude is to see the good fortune we have simply to be alive, to occupy the bodies we have, and to be able to see the beauty in the world around us.

In your own life, ask yourself what kind of role gratitude plays for you.
What are you most grateful for in your life? Do you feel yourself to be lucky?
Are you in the habit of saying thank you for what life has given you?
Can you see the benefits of gratitude playing out in your own life?

NOTE DOWN ANY THOUGHTS THAT COME TO MIND AND COMPLETE THIS OVER THE COMING WEEK.

....
....
....
....
....
....
....
....
....
....
....

A small book of thanks

We don't need to wait for something to happen to be able to say "thanks." We can just be grateful at any time, effortlessly. Mind you, simply saying the words "thank you" is not going to be enough. If we really want to see things change, we have to think about what we mean and put our hearts into it. Suppose we develop the habit of feeling grateful every single day. The best time to practice is at the start of the day, to say thanks for all the things that lie ahead, and then again at the end of the day. We can even share these acts of gratitude with those close to us.

Today, choose a new notebook, and write in it some of the best moments of gratitude you have experienced in your life.

Describe them in detail, so that you can start to feel what it was like for you at the time. Now take a look at your life today. Think about the path you have taken since you were born, and note down all the things for which you can be grateful: events, friends, loved ones, trips you made, people you met… Add to your notebook as often as you can over the following days, and over the coming months—and even years! Keep it close by, and on days when you feel you need a bit of a boost, open it up and read, realizing just how many good things are already in your life.

Gratitude and creativity

Remembering this sense of gratitude during our creative moments is a powerful technique, and can give us a real boost. Rather than feeling like victims of what life throws at us, we can feel as though life is giving us a helping hand—that life, in a sense, is on our side. Gratitude can help us de-stress, recover our creative vision, and realize the resources we have within ourselves. And the creative work we do becomes more pleasurable, as gratitude allows us to be more present, more centered, and more joyful. The positive energy that derives from our gratitude opens up new opportunities. Being able to give thanks for each small thing can create a feeling of prosperity, and by concentrating on what we have (rather than what we want) we are sending a message out inviting life to bring us more.

By feeling grateful before starting our creative activities, we can quickly generate an ideal atmosphere for creativity. How about giving it a go? Could you thank creativity for paying you a visit? Or thank your projects? Who or what else could you be grateful for?

WHAT COULD YOU DO TO EXPRESS YOUR GRATITUDE?

A list of thanks

You can use writing to help experience some of your deepest gratitude. Make a list of everything you feel grateful for in your life, starting with the simplest things. Don't stop too much to think, just write what comes into your head, and keep on going until you start to feel a change in your mood.

Once you have completed the list, read it back out loud. If you find that this had no effect on you at all, then make yourself a new list—or go out and take a walk!

Thank you for ....

Thank you for ....

Thank you for ....

Thank you for ....

Thank you for ....

Thank you for ....

Thank you for ....

Thank you for ....

Thank you for ....

Thank you for ....

Thank you for ....

Thank you for ....

HOW DO YOU FEEL NOW?

....

....

....

....

....

....

Thanks for the trouble

Being able to say thank you to the difficulties that come our way can really transform how we feel about them. We start by accepting that these difficulties exist. Then, we become aware that they have a role to play in our lives in communicating a message to us. It is a liberating idea. The following stage consists of thanking these difficulties for their existence as hidden gifts that have been bestowed on our lives. None of this makes the difficulties go away, but it does allow us to be more relaxed about them, so that new answers and solutions may emerge more easily.

ARE YOU FACING A PARTICULAR DIFFICULTY?

Can you describe it? How could you express gratitude for this particular difficulty? What "hidden gift" might lie at the heart of the problem you face? Will this help you reinforce your own self-love or self-confidence? What can you say thank you for and what could you learn? What are the positives in the situation as you see it right now?

....
....
....
....
....
....
....
....
....
....
....
....
....
....
....
....
....
....
....

A letter of thanks

The act of writing can help reinforce our sense of gratitude. So for today's exercise, you're going to write a letter of thanks—to yourself! You can say thanks for the path that you've chosen, for having courage, and for daring to go further than you thought possible. Thank yourself for your perseverance and creativity, for the support you have given yourself, and for your growing sense of self-love.

WHAT WOULD YOU LIKE TO ADD? NOW, MAIL IT TO YOURSELF!

If you would like to take this exercise further, you could write a letter addressed to your biggest difficulty, or pain, or illness. You could try thanking it for having come into your life, and for teaching you everything you have discovered about its existence.

....
....
....
....
....
....
....
....
....
....
....
....

A ritual for gratitude

Today, you are going to invent your own unique ritual for gratitude. Close your eyes and invite your inner child to join with you in this creative task. Now ask yourself, how would such a ritual look? And where will it take place? At your house? By the sea? At what time of day, or night? How will the ritual work? Perhaps you would like to dance, sing, or simply put your hands over your heart. Make a list of all that you feel grateful for, everything you would like to include in this ritual.

NOTE YOUR THOUGHTS, AND GET STARTED PLANNING THIS RITUAL TODAY. THEN WRITE ABOUT HOW IT WENT.

The capacity for wonder

Rediscovering wonder

DAY 338

Wonder is the capacity to see the beauty and magic in all the small things that surround us, and it feels rather like being a child again, as if we are seeing things for the very first time. It is about seeing the poetry of life in our daily lives, and it connects us with enthusiasm, dynamism, and joy. Above all, it is a powerful fuel for our creativity.

DO YOU HAVE A SENSE OF WONDER?

Do you find it easy, or difficult, to have this sense of wonder? Do you feel able to capture the magic of life? Can you remember the last time you felt this sense of wonder? What started it off? Are there times when you feel something is really "magical," and why do you think that is? What do you feel at the time? How did you experience a sense of wonder when you were a child? Suppose you were to look at life now through the spirit of that child, what would it change for you? What might it bring you? And what do these questions make you think and feel?

TAKE SOME TIME TO DESCRIBE IN DETAIL SOME OF YOUR MOST POWERFUL MOMENTS OF WONDER.

A day of wonder

Try to view your life and your surroundings through the eyes of your inner child.
They can find wonder in a flower, or a dragonfly, or a ladybird, or a smile, or a flash
of lightning. By cultivating a sense of wonder at the world around us, we can make
life seem more beautiful. If we decide to see gloom and grayness, that is what we
will see. Conversely, if we prepare ourselves to see beauty, we will find beauty.

Now take a deep breath and make a pledge that you will seize every possible
moment to find wonder in what you perceive. Imagine you're looking through the
eyes of your inner child.

Throughout the day, note down when you feel this sense of wonder emerging—
anything that seems to have a touch of the magical about it. Do you see beauty
and wonder in your environment? At the end of the day, read over your notes. Are
you surprised at what you wrote down? Do you feel anything changing inside you?

HOW DO YOU FEEL NOW?

Creative magic

Sometimes, right in the middle of our most creative moments, we can be touched by an incredible sensation when everything comes together: time stands still, and we feel disconnected from our minds. We experience an extreme sense of well-being, yet we are fully involved in what we are doing. This happened to me once, when I was painting a landscape outdoors. I felt totally in the moment of what I was doing, as if I actually *was* the paintbrush, the paper, the landscape. Time stood still. It was a moment of purity that has never returned to me again, but it was one of the best moments in my creative life. When I experience such moments, where both magic and wonder seem to be present, I give thanks, knowing well how rare and precious these moments are.

HAVE YOU EVER EXPERIENCED A SENSATION LIKE THIS, WHERE TIME SEEMS TO STAND STILL?

A sensation that makes you wonder where it came from? As if your work were being guided by an invisible hand? Write about the most "magical" experience of this kind you ever had, whether linked with creativity or a completely different aspect of your life. What was the experience like? And what do you think it was communicating to you?

....
....
....
....
....
....
....
....
....
....
....
....
....
....
....

The magic of the creative process

There is something magical about the creative process, in the sense that when we stop trying too hard—when we let go—that is when the ideas really begin to flow. So many times in my own experience, when I have felt stuck, or that things were just not working out, I would just try harder and harder. But then, I found that by doing the opposite—letting go, thinking about other things—the solution to my problem would appear. We can see this magic, too, in those little coincidences that happen to us, when things happen at the right time and in the right place, suddenly sowing the seeds of a new idea.

The good news is that we can all create the conditions to bring this magic into our lives. It needs fertile ground to land on—which we can provide by maximizing a sense of joy, relaxation, letting go, gratitude, and love in our daily lives, inviting the magic to come in.

HOW DO YOU WELCOME MAGIC INTO YOUR LIFE?

Do you have any particular memories of this? How do you express wonder in your own projects? How could you cultivate this further? Note down any ideas that come to you, and watch how things go over the next few days. Who knows what kind of magic might turn up?

....
....
....
....
....
....
....
....
....
....
....
....
....
....
....
....

Magical powers

With a sense of wonder at everything in the world, your inner child will adore magic. So why not bring your inner child along with you today?

IF YOU HAD MAGICAL POWERS, WHAT WOULD THEY BE?

And why? What would you use them to do? What aspects of your life would you change as a result? And how would you use them in your creative life?

....
....
....
....
....
....
....

Suppose you wrote a fairy tale to read to your inner child, in which they had magical powers. What kind of magical powers would they be? And what would it be like to live with those powers? If you feel in the mood, you could decorate your story with drawings or collage.

....
....
....

Wonder and creativity

Do you think some artists have a special talent to transmit their magic to us? Which painters, photographers, singers, musicians, chefs, or other creatives express a kind of magic that really speaks to you? How can these artists inspire you to put a sense of magic and wonder into your own creative work?

Take time to research some artists and makers, and find some of their work that really seems to connect with you. Where will you look? Maybe you will be able to find some images of these works, which you could print out, or even better, put up on your wall. Next time you set out to work on your own projects, take time to look at them and be inspired!

WHAT IDEAS DO YOU FIND INSPIRING? NOTE DOWN WHAT COMES UP, AND BE READY TO ADD MORE AS THE WEEK GOES ON.

....
....
....
....
....
....
....
....
....
....
....
....

Creative dreaming

Lie down, close your eyes, put on some inspiring music, and let yourself be carried by the flight of your imagination. If anything were possible, how could you add magic and wonder to your daily life? And what would the creative life of your dreams look like? Note down whatever comes to mind—even the strangest and weirdest ideas.

HOW DID IT GO? WHAT WAS THIS MAGICAL DREAM LIKE?
Plan to reread your ideas in two days' time, and see if some of these could find their way into your next creative project. Who knows?

....
....
....
....
....
....
....
....
....
....
....

Celebration

Congratulations!

So here we are, almost at the end of the book, and it's time for some congratulations. You can be really proud of yourself. Do you realize the kind of journey you have made since the beginning of this book? It's huge! So this week's section is going to be all about joy and celebration, and how much that plays a role in your life. Do you find it easier to encourage and celebrate with others than you do with yourself? Do you make time to congratulate yourself after some kind of victory (however small)? Do you take a moment to reward yourself and enjoy times when you have done something brilliantly? If you don't, why not? Supposing you did decide to celebrate your victories, what would that change? What was your most recent success? How could you celebrate that? Maybe you could give yourself a gift, spend time with a friend, have a massage, buy a beautiful notebook, take some creative time, or go see a movie. Or maybe do something you have been dreaming of doing for a long time. Write down your thoughts and make a list you can use in the future when you want to celebrate. Try not to filter your ideas, just get it all down on paper. What could you choose for today?

How far you've come

Knowing how to celebrate the successes in our lives makes us feel good about ourselves. By being proud of ourselves, and aware of our progress, we are encouraged to go even further. By celebrating our victories, we are celebrating ourselves. And we deserve it! We can be grateful, we can feel joy, and we can be proud of ourselves. So enjoy the feeling of success and the happiness it brings.

> TAKE A LOOK AT THE PATH YOU HAVE TAKEN SINCE BEGINNING THIS BOOK, AND OVER THE LAST 5 YEARS AND 10 YEARS. SEE WHERE YOU HAVE COME FROM, AND WHERE YOU WERE, BACK THEN.

What events or progress would you like to celebrate? How about celebrating the various *stages* of your creative projects, instead of just at the end point? How do you feel about how you've been changing? Does it make you want to go further? How would you like to celebrate where you are today?

How about illustrating the path you have been following? Draw a picture of it. Is it rough, twisting, rocky, long, steep? Maybe you can add details along the way, like people, trees, words, or symbols.

WHERE WOULD YOU PLACE YOURSELF ON YOUR CREATIVE PATH?

....
....
....
....
....
....
....
....
....
....
....
....
....
....
....
....

Be proud of yourself

Having moments when we feel we have really excelled can give us pride, confidence, and inner strength, and is a great benefit to our creativity. And if we can really celebrate these awesome moments, then we will gain the joy and enthusiasm to push even further. Suppose we could make a habit of these small personal celebrations. We could, for example, create small challenges each day that, when achieved, can give us a sense of satisfaction. It does not have to be something complex and difficult, but simply something where you have to push yourself a little bit further, that you recognize and celebrate. You will even be generating dopamine in your brain—the motivation hormone!

WHAT CHALLENGE COULD YOU GIVE YOURSELF TODAY?

And in which area? Relationships? Work? Cooking? Sport? Your creative project? Making an important phone call? Writing an email? Let your imagination go and see what comes up. Choose one to do now, and plan the others for each day of the coming week, or even the next month. How did you feel after completing each challenge? How did you, or how will you, celebrate?

....
....
....
....
....
....
....
....
....
....
....
....
....
....
....
....
....

Give thanks

Congratulating ourselves is a way of giving thanks for the talents that we have. We can give ourselves the recognition we deserve, without relying on others—or being dependent on it. Think of some reasons to be proud of yourself and why.

> I (NAME)…
> CONGRATULATE MYSELF FOR…

....
....
....
....
....
....
....
....
....
....
....
....

WHEN YOU'RE DONE, READ YOUR LIST OUT LOUD. HOW DO YOU FEEL NOW? HAS ANYTHING CHANGED? IF YES, WHAT EXACTLY?

....
....
....
....
....
....
....

Paying compliments

Most of us can think of times in our childhood when we felt a bit disappointed not to have gotten more support or encouragement in what we were doing. Our inner child may still feel hurt by these experiences. And whatever may have happened back then, by supporting and fostering the creativity of our own inner child today, we can help feel happier and more enthusiastic as adults. So close your eyes and call to mind your inner child, and congratulate them for all the creativity that they have shown in accompanying you on your creative journey. Can you give some examples? What encouraging things could you tell them? Say the words you would have liked to hear when you were a child.

WHAT WAS THAT LIKE FOR YOU? HOW ARE YOU FEELING NOW?

....
....
....
....
....
....
....
....
....
....
....
....

Sharing the glory

Celebrating the creative work of our friends and colleagues can make us feel great. By supporting them on their creative journey, we are helping ourselves at the same time. By taking the credit for our own success, while doing the same for others, we are not only providing a mutual sense of recognition, but we are also helping to build a solid foundation for our own creativity.

HOW ABOUT MEETING UP WITH A FEW OF YOUR CREATIVE FRIENDS?

You could organize a party to celebrate your creativity as a group. Who would you invite? How and when could you do this? Maybe you could plan regular meet-ups like this? What steps could you take today to get this started? Write down any ideas that come to you, and then call your friends to discuss it.

....
....
....
....
....
....
....

ATTACH A PHOTO OF YOUR GET-TOGETHER HERE

The pleasure of celebrating life

Today, I'd like you to think about celebrating life itself, the simple fact of being alive, and your own special attributes that make you who you are—including, of course, your talents and creativity. You deserve it! Look at what you have done and who you are. Celebrate your creative energy, the unique experiences you have lived—or even just celebrate this present moment. It is simple but valuable, and will give you a richer sense of your creative life.

HOW DO YOU FEEL ABOUT THIS IDEA?

What would you like to celebrate today? And how? And when? Take another look at the list of celebrations that you began at the start of this week (Day 345), and maybe add more. Which one will you choose?

....
....
....
....
....
....
....
....
....
....
....
....
....
....
....
....
....
....

WEEK 51
The best of endings

DAY 352

The problem with endings

It's not always easy to finish a project in which we have invested so much of our love and energy. In fact, I sometimes find that I want to slow things down as I get toward the end of a project because it has become something very close to my heart, occupying an important part of my life. Luckily, this kind of nostalgia eventually gives way to an eagerness to simply move on to something completely new. It is right here that we can see more clearly than ever that even if a project must come to an end, the creative process itself goes on as a continuous cycle. By learning how to finish something, we are creating space to welcome in something new.

What is it like for you, coming to the end of your projects? Do you find it hard? Which projects have you managed to finish? What benefits do you see from finishing projects—and what downsides? How could you motivate yourself more to reach the end of your projects? Could you try imposing deadlines, for example? Or maybe get a creatively minded friend to help you out?

NOTE DOWN YOUR IDEAS, AND SEE WHICH ONES WOULD BE THE SIMPLEST TO PUT IN PLACE.

....
....
....
....
....
....
....
....
....
....
....
....
....
....
....

Time to review

A creative review is a great way to finish a project and to feel a real sense of satisfaction from the work you have done. By drawing out learning points, and getting a sense of the progress made, we can stimulate our creativity even further while readying ourselves for the next creative adventure.

Here is a list of questions that might help you in reviewing your work, drawing widely on your own creative life and the work you have done within this book too. Of course, you can adapt these questions to suit any kind of project.

Read back over the list of your hopes and expectations that you wrote in this book on Day 1, and get a sense of the path you have traveled. What have you learned about yourself and others? Have you achieved what you intended to? If not, why? Have your objectives evolved? How? What is your lasting impression of this year of creativity? Has it been a positive experience? Can you say how? What creative experience has left the biggest impression on you this year? What new skills have you learned? What was the best moment? How have your creative projects advanced during this time? How have they helped you evolve?

What are you most proud of, since starting out with this book? What made you happiest during this year—which experience in particular? And why? The more detail you manage to put into describing what happened, the more you will find value in what you have done. What can you be most proud of? Think back to where you were when you began this book. Have you noticed any changes within yourself?

CONGRATULATIONS! YOU CAN BE PROUD OF YOURSELF!

Your new vision of creativity

Since starting this book, it's likely that your view of creativity has changed, though maybe you have not been fully aware of this. Today, I would like you read back over the answers you gave during Week 2, and see if you can see an evolution in your thinking. Where are you now, in terms of your relationship with creativity, compared with where you were at the start of this book? Has anything changed, and if so, what? What have you become more aware of? What beliefs have you been able to cast aside? And what new beliefs have you taken on board? Do you see yourself as more creative than before? Do you feel more confident? Do you feel the flow of creative energy? How do you feel about blocks and difficulties? How do you feel, generally, about how things are evolving?

TAKE YOUR TIME WITH YOUR ANSWERS— AND APPRECIATE THE DISTANCE YOU HAVE TRAVELED.

Going even further

Even if we can see progress in so many aspects of our creative lives, this does not mean that we have now "arrived" at our destination and we can't go any further. Creativity is dynamic, never static, and is constantly pushing us forward to new things.

If you were to start this book again at the beginning, what would you do differently? Would you choose to explore something else? What new thing could you try, even if it was way harder than you imagined? What mistakes do you think you made, and what did they teach you? Does this make you want to push on even further?

Today, take some time to read back through your answers throughout this book and in your notebook. Can you spot any themes or preoccupations? What message can you draw from these?

WRITE DOWN ANY THEMES THAT EMERGE. WHAT DO THEY EVOKE IN YOU? COULD THESE SPARK OFF NEW PROJECTS? WRITE WHATEVER COMES TO MIND.

Taking stock

Take another look at the exercises in Week 5, starting from where you are now. In which area of your life do you think you have made the most progress in terms of creativity?

Now take a sheet of paper and some colored pens, and do a mind map (see Day 66), reviewing this year of creativity, in the areas that you have chosen to focus on and through the projects that you have worked on. Use some of your answers over the last few days to help you. Add some cute drawings if you like.

TAKE A LOOK AT YOUR MIND MAP. WHAT STRIKES YOU?

	SCORE
HEALTH	
FAMILY	
WORK	
FINANCES	
INTIMATE RELATIONSHIPS	
SEXUALITY	
FRIENDSHIP	
SOCIAL INTERACTIONS	
SPIRITUALITY	
WELL-BEING	

....
....
....
....
....
....

Clearing the decks

To bring about a really nice, clean ending to a project, we can also do a really nice, clean job of sorting out our work space. I love the process of sorting out the different bits of paper, ideas, art reference, you name it, that were involved in a project—keeping some, tossing others—and then tidying up my work space, which really gives me a sense that something has been completed. What's more, this provides a fresh, uncluttered space to start thinking about new things.

Are you in the habit of sorting out and cleaning up when a project comes to an end? What needs sorting out, do you think? Ideas, papers, notes? When you do this, perhaps you find unused ideas that could be useful in another project. How does this clearing out make you feel? Note down what comes to mind.

....
....
....
....
....
....
....
....

A ritual for closure

Can you think of how you might like—symbolically—to finish this stage in your creative life: coming to the end of this book about creativity? Perhaps you would like to invent your own ritual, to help let go of this project that has been running alongside your life for this past year. Close your eyes and call on your inner child to inspire you with ideas. What could you imagine doing?

WRITE DOWN YOUR IDEAS AND, WHEN YOU HAVE COMPLETED YOUR RITUAL, WRITE ABOUT THE EXPERIENCE.

Ready for a new beginning?

DAY 359

Preparing the transition

Coming to the end of a creative project can feel a bit weird, especially if it is a big project. Sometimes I have found myself working 10 to 15 hours a day on a project to hit a deadline, and then found that once it was complete, I felt totally lost with nothing else to do—as if I had been racing around a hamster wheel and it suddenly came to an abrupt stop. I can still see myself pacing around my work room, unable to concentrate on anything, feeling absolutely drained, but also still buzzing with too much creative energy to be able to rest. What I had failed to do was think of any kind of transition between projects.

Have you felt a sense of loss after finishing a project? Have you found yourself so attached to a project that you made no plans for what happened afterward? How do you manage the transitions between your projects? What could you do to better prepare for this transition? Do you have ideas for future projects? In which direction do you want to take them? You could do a mind map of your creative options, and maybe it's time to start a new notebook.

NOTE DOWN YOUR IDEAS AND CHOOSE ONE FOR TODAY.

A creative vacation

Sometimes, the best we can do at the end of an intense creative project is simply take some time for ourselves. It can be great to give ourselves time to regenerate, with no demands or expectations: just to enjoy life and make the most of some free time, in a genuine phase of creative rest and recreation.

Perhaps your needs and aspirations have shifted. Perhaps you could simply read a good book, listen to some music (and maybe dance), see a movie, get a massage, walk in a forest, sign up for a new course, have a party …

Start by doing something you enjoy, however simple. Call up your inner child and get them to help. What would they like to do? How could you recharge your batteries and take care of yourself? Note down any new ideas. What could you do today?

WHAT COULD YOU GET STARTED OVER THE COMING DAYS?

....
....
....
....
....
....
....
....
....
....
....
....
....
....

Return to what you love

When you want to prepare for a fresh start on a new project, one of the best ways to do so is to bring the focus back to the things you're passionate about. The creative cycle has come full circle, the job is done, and we can now break through to a higher level of creativity, enriched by what has gone before. By concentrating on the things we love the most, we are returning to our true selves: it is fertile ground for ideas. Reread the answers you gave to the themes in Weeks 12 and 17, and see if some of the thoughts still resonate.

NOTE THEM HERE, AND LET THEM SINK IN SLOWLY.

....
....
....
....
....
....
....
....
....
....
....
....
....
....

Best of the best

Throughout this book, you will have come across dozens of different kinds of creative exercises. Today's task is to pick out the exercises you feel worked best for you, so you can make your own personalized recipe book of creative activities. Dip into it whenever you feel the need, with exercises you can turn to at any stage in the creative process.

What exercises did you find the most inspiring? Which gave you the most energy? Which did you like the most, and which gave you a new kind of awareness? Perhaps some helped you persevere at a difficult moment. Others may have helped you through a creative block. Maybe you can create your own bespoke exercises.

START YOUR LIST HERE.

....
....
....
....
....
....
....
....
....
....

DRAW A GRID SHOWING YOUR FAVORITE EXERCISES FROM THIS BOOK,
AND DECORATE IT USING COLORS, DRAWINGS OR COLLAGE. ONCE IT'S DONE,
KEEP IT IN YOUR CREATIVE HAPPY BOX.

What's in your box?

Did you keep using your creative happy box over the course of the year? Perhaps now is the time to take a fresh look at it as you prepare for your next creative journey. How could you adapt it to make it more useful for some of your future projects? Maybe you could take out what you no longer need and add some new objects or images that make you feel good. Make sure you include lists (and photos) of the people and things most important to you, along with drawings, lists, and any newfound treasures and inspiration. Feeling down? Go check out your happy box! It's there for you—and full of your most inspirational things.

Remember also to complete your gratitude notebook and to read what you've written there: it will make your heart sing!

HOW DID IT GO?

....
....
....
....
....
....
....
....
....
....
....

A message from the future

Today, I'd like you to imagine your creative self in the future. Start by thinking about who you were just one year ago, how far you've come creatively, and then imagine who you would like to be, in a creative sense, in one year's time.

Think about who you would like to become. Write yourself a letter from your future creative self. What would they say to you? How will they be living their creative life?

ONCE THE LETTER IS WRITTEN, READ IT OUT LOUD. HOW DO YOU FEEL NOW?

....
....
....
....
....
....
....
....
....
....
....
....

The last word

YOU MADE IT! YOU GOT ALL
THE WAY TO THE END!

How will you celebrate the end of this incredible year of creativity?
Perhaps last week's exercises (on celebrations) gave you some ideas.
Pick your favorite idea from last week's list and do it!

....

....

....

....

I'd love for you to continue on this creative path, cultivating your passion
and enthusiasm as you go, and finding ideas that allow you to put your
passions into practice. Your creativity will blossom,
filling you with joy and gratitude.

It has been an honor for me to join you on this path, and I want to give you
my sincere thanks. I wish you the very best for your future creative life.
This book marks an ending: but you are about to make a new beginning!

AND NOW, IT'S OVER TO YOU!

A bonus

Close your eyes. Imagine the inspirational presence of creativity in the distance,
as a person, a luminous essence, an angel, a star: the form or the image does not
matter. Now imagine a rainbow full of sparkling colors, standing between creativity and
you. Walk toward it, until you arrive at the base. Take a step and walk beneath the rainbow,
sharply aware of your innermost feelings. Now continue walking joyfully and confidently
to the other side of the rainbow. Creativity is right there. Imagine that it wraps you in an
embrace, full of creative energy that quickly mixes with your own, dissolving into every cell
of your body. All those creative qualities become you, running through your being, and you
become pure creativity. Take a moment to reflect on all these sensations, and the effect they
have on you … before setting off on your new creative life!

ACKNOWLEDGMENTS

First of all, a big thank you to all of you!

Thank you to Adeline, my editor, whose support and enthusiasm allowed this fabulous project to come to life. Thank you to Christine for reading so carefully through my early draft, and for being such a good friend for such a long time. Thank you to Anne, Michèle, and Ophélie, my EPR creative team, for working on this project with such enthusiasm. Thank you to Shelby and the girls for your friendship and encouragement. Thank you to Damien, for the truly creative page layouts.And thank you to my family, friends, and soul mates: without you, I would not be here.

BIBLIOGRAPHY

The Artist's Way: A Spiritual Path to Higher Creativity, by Julia Cameron. TarcherPerigee, 2002.

Big Magic: Creative Living Beyond Fear, by Elizabeth Gilbert. Riverhead Books, 2016.

Mind Map Mastery: The Complete Guide to Learning and Using the Most Powerful Tool in the Universe, by Tony Buzan. Watkins Publishing, 2018.

Créez la Vie Qui Vous Ressemble, by Anne-Marie Jobin. Éditions de l'Homme, 2018.

Steal Like an Artist: 10 Things Nobody Told You About Being Creative, by Austin Kleon. Workman Publishing, 2012.

Wake up!: 4 Principes Fondamentaux pour Arrêter de Vivre Sa Vie à Moitié Endormi, by Christine Lewicki. Eyrolles, 2014.

Ask and It Is Given: Learning to Manifest Your Desires, by Esther and Jerry Hicks. Hay House Inc., 2004.

English translation: Paul Carslake

Editorial director: Thierry Lamarre
Editor: Adeline Lobut
Concepts and text: Ghylenn Descamps
Design and layout: Either studio/Damien Payet
Cover design: Diane Lamphron
Illustrations: ©Shutterstock

Published in English in 2020 by Get Creative 6, an imprint of Mixed Media Resources, 104 West 27th Street, Third Floor, New York, NY 10001
Connect with us on Facebook at facebook.com/getcreative6

Original title:
365 jours pour libérer sa créativité © 2018 by Éditions Marie Claire - Société d'Information et Créations (SIC)

CIP data available upon request.

ISBN: 978-1-68462-010-4

Manufactured in China

1 3 5 7 9 10 8 6 4 2

First English Edition